The *Everyday God*

Changing Lives at Home and at Work

The Everyday God

Changing Lives at Home and at Work

Jack Dominian
and Edmund Flood

GEOFFREY
CHAPMAN

Geoffrey Chapman

An imprint of Cassell Publishers Limited
Villiers House, 41/47 Strand, London WC2N 5JE
378 Park Avenue South, New York, NY 10016–8810

First published 1993

British Library Cataloguing-in-Publication Data
A catalogue record for this book is available from the British
Library.

Library of Congress Cataloging-in-Publication Data
Available from the Library of Congress.

ISBN 0–225–66676–6

Typeset by Colset Private Limited, Singapore
Printed and bound in Great Britain by
Biddles Ltd, Guildford and King's Lynn

Contents

Acknowledgements

We would particularly like to thank Ruth McCurry, our publisher's Religious Editor, for outstanding help at all stages of our writing this book.

The following kindly gave Edmund Flood interviews, for which he would like to thank them: Jean Balcombe (Industrial Society), Clive Beck (Mowlem), Elizabeth Bradley (Girls Friendly Society), Lavinia Byrne IBVM (Inter-Church House), Joseph Carter and Kevin Flanagan (St Anthony's Centre for Church and Industry), Nevill Clifford-Jones, Quentin de la Bedoyère, Brian Fairweather (Age Concern), Gerry Flanagan and friends (YCW, Salford), Michael Garvey (Ministry to the Disabled, Archdiocese of Westminster), John Haughey SJ (Loyola University, Chicago), Douglas Hollis (Department of the Environment), Anne Leeming (City of London Business School), Michael Little, Charles Moore (formerly of John Grooms Association for Disabled People), Sir Richard O'Brien (Church Urban Fund), Stephen O'Brien (Business in the Community), Greg Pierce (formerly Director, National Center for the Laity, USA), John Pierce (Church Action on Disability), Michelle Rigby (London Churches Employment Development Unit), Nancy E. Robertson (formerly of Prince of Wales Advisory Group on Disability), John Swain (business consultant), Michael White (Policy Studies Institute) and Peter and Patricia Worden.

He would like also to thank the following libraries and their librarians: Industrial Society, London Business School, Policy Studies Institute, Notre Dame University (and kind hospitality from the Notre Dame community, which was much enjoyed).

Jack Dominian
Edmund Flood

Part Two is by Jack Dominian; Parts One, Three, Four and Five are by Edmund Flood, as are the Reflections and prayer notes at chapter ends.

PART ONE
THE GOOD NEWS IS FOR ALL

What do people want from the churches?

Survey after survey shows that the great majority believe in God. They believe that there is a transcendental force that could give our lives meaning.

When they look at their main activities, their family and work lives, they see developments that can make them much more humanly fulfilling. Instead of being largely impersonal, both may be becoming increasingly personal. Today you are more likely to find an attempt to share, to treat as equal, to show you care for the other.

But belief in God, and this greater chance of a human kind of meaning, usually remain on separate tracks. God is for church-going and some major crises, but much less for every day. As a result, surveys also show great disenchantment with the churches. They are widely seen as marginal in our quest for meaning.

Jesus' gospel of good news

But Christianity started for only one reason. Jesus discovered and proclaimed the good news at the centre of our lives. Most good news is superficial or fades or is about a possible tomorrow. Jesus' good news was about the very meaning and fulfilment of our everyday lives.

You may be a homemaker or a salesperson; you may be a manager or retired: whatever you mainly do, and in whatever context, you are trying to live as your true self. 'You will achieve that', Jesus was saying, 'with an unimaginable fullness. From your "sowing" an immense harvest; from your "fishing" an immense catch. Committing yourself to this enterprise is the best thing you could ever do.'

This wasn't just a theory or a hunch: it was already happening through his actions. Foul, blind beggars in the market-place recovered their sight. Prostitutes and toll-collectors recovered their dignity and their sense of belonging. He helped each towards healing and wholeness.

The extraordinary claims Jesus made for his actions arose from his own experience. What made those actions of healing and wholeness possible was not just human power but God's power. At the heart of his experience was the transforming power of a loving 'Father' working through him to fulfil people's deepest needs.

It is only from out of our deepest, everyday needs that we can understand the news he gives us. One of our needs is *to experience the joy of being alive because someone loves us.* Many people feel desperately deprived of that experience. 'Why should I go on living?' is a question that a psychiatrist is frequently asked by his or her clients. 'What you can see at the heart of all I am and all I do', Jesus was saying, 'is a God who loves you. My true followers are those who share in showing that love to all.'

Another of our needs is to experience *a human quality in our relationships*. In Jesus' healings, and in his warm hospitality and kindness, Jesus believed that God's transforming power (or 'Kingdom') was creating that quality.

We also need *to feel ourselves as loving*. We need to feel ourselves knowing and responding to the goodness of others and to feel involved in the business of human life: the business of being involved with others. Such loving was Jesus' one command and purpose.

Only when these three needs are met can I experience my life as creative and fulfilling.

Jesus' one message was that God's transforming power fulfilling these needs had now come in its fullness. To a Jew that could only mean the breaking-in of the new world God had promised when all would be transformed. 'Father, may your transforming power (or "Kingdom") come' was both his prayer and his promise.

It was a ridiculous message, by almost anyone's standards. His contemporaries, living in a cruelly occupied country, laughed at such a claim. Jesus, also, knew intimately the cruelty and poverty. He knew about evil and the human havoc it was causing and the threat it posed to his own life. Even so, he announced that in the transformed world that was now beginning evil could not win.

Jesus' invitation wasn't just to *receive* this good news but to *enjoy making it real for others*. Would it be the good news of a lifetime if it made us passive receivers like infants? Jesus' invitation to his friends was to be partners. He rejoiced in his power to create, through whatever danger and effort, a renewed world. But his greatest joy was that his friends would be co-creators of this transformed world.

The strength and range of Jesus' work became clearer after he had risen. His community would make him and his work accessible. To a Christian, this community, the church, is the central drama in our world's history. To join in its work is 'the pearl of great price' for which all someone's wealth can be sacrificed.

Pale versions of Jesus' gospel

Just as a government administrator may see the reality of the Health Service as committees, budgets and policy statements while the rest of us see it in terms of nurses, doctors and hospitals, so Christians have tended to see the church institution that serves this central drama as the only thing that really matters, not the human meaning and fulfilment that come from loving in each person's life.

The result is not just that non-Christians are left out of the drama, but also that the good news itself is seen from a radically false perspective. It becomes a pale version of Jesus' gospel, as many Christians now recognize. For Christians, this institution, the church, can become largely a haven: an escape into a 'religious' world exclusive to themselves. It ceases to be about the world God so loved that he sent his Son to save it: the world of human relationships in family, work and the wider society. Perhaps the world is right to be critical of the church?

In the 1990s it is especially urgent for us to recapture the biblical perspectives. As we approach the year 2000, there is a growing mood of wanting to prepare for a fresh and livelier start in the new millennium. To focus on evangelism (= 'bringing the good news') could concentrate our minds on what Christianity can really offer. Calling the 1990s the Decade of Evangelization or Evangelism was therefore a stroke of genius.

But at the moment the results are acknowledged to be very meagre.

3

When someone suggested to an experienced pastor that the decade is running out of steam, he denied this. 'The decade has never *had* any steam', he said. 'Most people didn't know what it meant in the first place.'

In this book we shall use Scripture, church teaching, and the world we live in to show the opportunity that lies before us of rediscovering God in our everyday world.

How the Bible sees *all* people

Is this good news just for Christians? If you live in China or Afghanistan where the church is almost absent, or if you live in the West but have had no real chance to know what Jesus was really like or what he meant by 'God', must you miss all that God can give? We are talking, on current estimates, of thousands of millions of our contemporaries. Can the God who created the whole world have nothing to give those great numbers of people who are outside the church's reach?

By regaining the Bible's perspectives we don't just rescue ourselves from this contradiction. We also achieve a clearer view of the human relevance of the good news and of the role of the church.

The Old Testament focuses on the central drama of the life of the People in whom God was particularly present. Even so, its editors wanted to put that drama into true perspective. Like many an editor since, they used a preface for that purpose.

Their preface (the first chapters of Genesis) shows us that God's involvement in the human story is much wider than his relationship with his own People. *All* men and women, it says, are 'images' of God.

At first that statement may have little impact. An image can be as faint as an overexposed photograph. But nothing faint was intended by the writer. In Hebrew it meant that women and men are intended to be 'human projections' of God. Women and men are 'in the most basic definition that which God becomes if he sets out to show himself in the region of the extra-divine' (Karl Rahner).

The Bible is saying that this is the calling of all human beings. It is what we essentially are, and what we are invited increasingly to become. What a human being is for, is to manifest God in this actual world where we are at home. That seems grandiose,

4

unrealistic, until we see how we're meant to do that. Just as God made things be and brings them fruitfulness, so must we. The 'God of tenderness and compassion, slow to anger, rich in kindness and faithfulness', as he revealed himself to Moses, became known through what he did: making things be, out of love. We are called to share in that responsible and loving creativity. 'Be fruitful and increase' wasn't just the command, but the opportunity for everyone.

We have only to test this claim that the human vocation is creativity, out of love, against our experience to recognize its validity. Whether people believe in God or not, don't we find that at the end of the day they judge themselves on their wholeness and fruitfulness? 'Am I a parent who acts true to myself and does my best for my children?' Whatever our main roles may happen to be, most of us would at least like to apply that kind of yardstick. 'Responsible creativity' or fruitfulness is generally what our yardstick consists of.

So God's good news is not an extra handout reserved for the religious. It consists, instead, in every person's vocation to become fully human. The ways we can fulfil that are as various as our roles in life. You may be retired or unemployed; you may be a parent or a nurse, a truck driver or a lawyer: the things you do and are responsible for are your world, and it's in that world that you join in God's work. It is often not in religion, but in the heart of our lives, that we glimpse God.

Before we continue to test this by our experience, we must first recall other key perceptions in that preface to Genesis. The most obvious is the goodness of the whole creation, in spite of that major flaw in our human aims and responses of which we are often conscious and which the story of the Fall portrays. Another is that a genuinely human life must be one of shared human intimacy. Another is our human solidarity in the human story.

Is it true that in seeking wholeness and fruitfulness in what we do we can glimpse a transcendent force at the heart of things? Is there a satisfaction and a power that can draw us on, to a level beyond our limited, fragile being? Is there a 'music heard so deeply / That it is not heard at all, but you are the music / While the music lasts' (T. S. Eliot, *The Dry Salvages*)?

At least at some times in our lives we can have such experiences. We react to a personal claim on us with a wholeheartedness that goes beyond all calculation. 'I can't tell you why I'm going to these

5

lengths to help this person, or to stand up for this value. I only know that I couldn't live with myself if I did not.'

Such a response is unlikely to be a momentary one. It will probably be a commitment we live out in our day to day existence. When we were planning this book together, Jack Dominian spoke about his thirty years of experience as a psychiatrist, helping many people. 'I have seen, in the course of my professional life, so much loving sacrifice: spouses dealing with depressed partners, or alcoholic partners; parents dealing with schizophrenic children. I've seen so much sanctity in totally unrecognized quarters of life. There is an immense amount of altruism in human behaviour.'

Another test of this claim that God is to be found at the centre of our most human actions, not in religion by itself, would be to consider what happens when we worship. The purpose of worship, in the Bible's view, is to deepen our joy and our commitment to our working with God in our human actions. The prophets denounced as bogus a worship which was a substitute for that. Of course we *can* get a satisfaction from a kind of worship that is a soothing escape from our human tasks. But don't we find that satisfaction to be radically different from one that genuinely arises from what we do, or share in doing?

Our church leaders have certainly recognized this momentous shift in Christian consciousness, that it is *in life* that God can be found. When they use 'Spirit of God' to express this, they can use that phrase as the Bible does: not to describe something that is nebulous or outside human experience, but 'God as he makes himself known' (Peter Carnley). Even a traditional leader like John Paul II declares that 'the Spirit is at work in the heart of every person . . . in human initiatives – including religious ones – and in man's efforts to attain truth, goodness and God himself' (John Paul II).

If God can be found in our efforts to attain truth and goodness, this might make joining a church seem to be unnecessary. In fact, the church has a vital role, as we shall see throughout this book. But we cannot recognize the real nature of that role until we realize that Christians have no monopoly of God's transforming presence. Christians have tended to believe or to assume that we *have* that monopoly. We've seen the good news as our exclusive possession: if non-Christians want any part of it, they can find it only in us, and they'll share in it only by joining us. People have found Scripture texts that seem to support that claim.

The result of taking that view is not just to cut off from the good news most of the world God loved. It is also to make that news unrecognizably different from the biblical vision of it.

The results of reducing the good news

All of us have experienced tenderness, compassion, kindness and faithfulness in people of other faiths or none. So if we think that the good news is exclusive to us Christians, it can't possibly be about that! That makes us think of Christianity as consisting of 'religious' things like rites, or beliefs in certain doctrines. This is not only a travesty of the attitude of Jesus and of the early Christian community, where people's life, humanity and love were the consuming concern. It also diverts our search for God from where the Bible, so insistently, tells us he can be found: in our common quest to make the life we all share more human, in our everyday world of family life and work.

Besides preventing us from recognizing God, that unbiblical view also cuts us off from the many people who should be our partners. In the organizations that matter to us, or in the place where we live, there are many who are not Christian and also want to make people's lives more human and fulfilled. The Christian reaction to these people has sometimes been to ignore them or to keep them at a distance, as though Christian activities and organizations were the only fully 'authentic' way to help. One result is that many Christians have to a large degree been deprived of the sense of involvement in the great enterprise of making life more human, where alone our good news can be found. Another result is that it has become much more difficult for Christians to be inspired by and collaborate with God's presence and goodness in the secular society, cutting us off from so much of God's good news or 'Kingdom'. The loss must be incalculable.

This massive impoverishment could quite quickly disappear. The churches could move from the margins to a central relevance. This does not depend on national committees or pronouncements, because the reality of a church is not primarily national. It is *in our different localities* that our lives are largely lived, and so it is in them that our churches count the most. You and I, in our localities, can change things all around, and this book suggests ways of bringing these changes about.

The church's role in the good news

When we think of our local church, in the light of our discussion, we realize that it operates in three ways.

First way Since it is in what we mainly do that we work with God and find him, and since this happens away from the church buildings, the main role of my church is to be *a kind of HQ for members*. Through worship and the Word of God, through church teaching and mutual Christian support, it should help us work with and find God in what we do 'out there'. Our church's main function is to help us find God in our actual and different lives.

Second way We know that a church has also a corporate reality. *We can act as a body*. There may be initiatives that local churches could take to help in this work of transformation.

Third way It is through both of these functions that a church, or a body of Christians, becomes what it is meant to be. Although every man and woman's essential calling is to be a manifestation or projection of God, it was Jesus Christ who showed God in his transforming power fully. The role of any church is to '*embody*', make generously accessible, *that fullness so far as it is able*. Through the individual and corporate lives of its members, its role is to show the locality what God really does.

Together these are the splendour of the church's vocation. That splendour does not consist in an escape into a rarefied apartness, or into something essentially different from any authentic life. It consists in an opportunity to be more creative and fruitful in our everyday human story. 'The Church is a means in God's hands to establish *shalom* [= wholeness] in this world' (J. C. Hoekendijk).

The Church is a *means* for that: it doesn't exist for its own sake. 'The primary reality is the Kingdom of God, and the function of the church makes no sense apart from it . . . The Church is never an end in itself' (Richard McBrien).

If the gospels are our inspiration, two great changes will happen. Our motivation will become much stronger and, above all, deeper; and we will be back in the real world, fired and helped by the goodness of many people and the reality of people's needs. 'We want to be a church-for-others slowly turning into the church-with-others', wrote another theologian (David Bosch).

The temptation will persist for all of us to take the much easier path of letting our Christianity exonerate us from 'the hard labour of love' for people in their needs. When we give in to that temptation, we see our church life as meaningful in independence from the total human community. When the church does that 'it betrays the major purpose of its existence' (John Baker).

Recognizing the everyday God

As we'll be seeing throughout this book, our society has a unique opportunity to make life for all of us increasingly personal: in our families, in our work, and in the way we tackle our social problems and opportunities. It is through grasping this opportunity that all of us can find God.

We've seen how Genesis shows that we are called to find God through our responsible and loving creativity: by being a good parent, marriage partner, workmate or neighbour. We know that how we handle these responsibilities is the test of our humanity. It is *there*, Genesis says, that God is at work and can be found. When we find joy and meaning in these responsibilities, we may not believe that this is an experience of God. What can especially open our eyes is reflection on our deepest experiences.

If I remain loyal to my spouse or child, even when they anger me or wrong me; if I sacrifice something I particularly value for my neighbour or workmate, though it brings me neither thanks nor recognition but simply being true to myself: when I do such things I'm being drawn by something that I cannot fathom but which exists at the centre of my life, even though it transcends me.

Or if I get home at the end of an 'impossible' day to find my spouse harshly critical and unsympathetic, and, nevertheless, show love. Or if I place the good of my fellow workers or employees before my own reputation or other advantage, or if I work for disadvantaged or dependent people without thought of reward, but in response to their lovableness and dignity: in such cases, too, I have found in people, by nature limited, something of absolute value. That value comes from the depth of them, and it calls to the depth of me. Although it transcends us both, it is the essence of loving relationships, utterly real and practical. It's what St Paul called 'the tough labour of love' (1 Thessalonians 1:3).

As well as in our particular relationships, this depth can be found in our noblest ideals. I want this to be a firm or family where all can fulfil themselves and feel cared for. I will fight this discrimination, deprivation, or other injustice. Here, again, I take full possession of my self in all my freedom and responsible creativity. My aim is to nourish the true 'self', the full humanity, of the people I seek to help. Here, too, the task is often arduous. But what draws me on is a value in my aim that is beyond any measurement. I may not succeed in my quest, but I know that abandoning the search would be a destruction of my real self.

This transcendence that we find beckoning us is what Scripture means by 'God'. It calls us to love *ourselves*: to find and to enjoy ourselves in the freedom and the fullness of our human response to others. It calls us to love '*the other*': in the full depth of their lovableness and need. It calls us to love the 'melody' we might call *God* that we discern in the call itself: telling of grace, telling of meaning, telling of inexhaustible fulfilment as a human being. Loving God, self and neighbour are, in Scripture, one.

It is this *common* experience, open to all, that this book seeks to explore, as we can find it in our everyday activities, whether we're Christian or not. So our subject is everybody's story. As Christians we do not have a different story. In Scripture's terms, all are called to be 'human projections of God'. What Scripture and the Christian life can do is to offer greater motivation for, and a stronger light on, the journey all feel called to take. Through their fellowship with Jesus Christ, the fullest 'human projection of God' (Hebrews 1:3), Christians *should* be better able to discern the harvest that beckons us and to commit themselves to reaping it with all who respond to the good news in them.

So we shall explore everybody's story, with attention, throughout, to how the church can fulfil its central task: to be a 'light' to all. Our exploration will look closely at the four chief areas of everyday life. The first is our most immediate experience of love and depth in the ups and downs of our closest relationships. The next is the great opportunities for work in firms, large and small, to become an experience of partnership in something humanly worthwhile: we will see how this can be brought about and why many fail to do this.

The third area of our exploration is another major opportunity that has been opened up to us in the last decades: that our retirement years can be the 'crown' of our lives. And the last area is the social needs of our time. We want our lives to make a difference. As ordinary citizens and as local churches, how can we achieve that? We look carefully at the needs and at what can be done to meet them.

Through such routes all of us find our true selves. As Christians we believe that by following them we find the everyday God.

PART TWO
MARRIAGE

Introduction

When we turn to most people's experience of marriage today, do we find a depth that we might call 'God'? It is common knowledge that the married lives of Christians are often no better than those of others. But what is the central insight that Christianity offers to everyone about marriage?

Marriage and God have been linked since the Old Testament. At the heart of contemporary marriage is a relationship of love between a man and a woman; and what happens within this relationship is for the majority of human beings their experience of God. Christians claim that all that God has revealed about his nature is summarized in the one word 'love', and so all that is expressed in love between husband and wife is living and experiencing God in practice.

Marriage begins with a commitment between a man and a woman to each other for life. This reflects the commitment in the nature of God expressed in the Trinity in terms of three persons in relationships of love with each other: a love that has no beginning and no end. When a couple make their commitment of love they enter this mystery of the life of God. They live this life of love by sustaining, healing and growing with each other.

They sustain each other through physical and emotional

13

availability. They make their selves a present to each other by being a gift which is slowly unwrapped in the successive stages of their relationship. The gift is themselves physically, emotionally and sexually available. They enjoy the beauty of each other's body, mind and soul. They feast on each other's generous availability.

But what is available is incomplete, as men and women are incomplete and wounded. The love they bear to each other has the capacity to be a healing power. In this sense they provide grace to each other just as God is constantly available to provide his grace to heal us. In so far as they heal each other they are encountering God in one another. This healing may be physical, emotional or spiritual.

Beyond sustaining and healing, a couple help each other to grow. They become responsible for each other's development. The most important development is emotional: enabling each other to grow in their capacity to love. To be patient, tolerant, understanding, sympathetic, considerate, forgiving, hopeful, persevering, trusting and faithful: all this takes a lifetime, and marriage is for the majority of human beings the school of love. They learn, year by year, to be as loving as God.

The inner world of married love is summarized in the ability of two people to sustain, heal and grow with each other. Subsequent chapters deal with the details of these events.

This inner world of marriage is sustained by the qualities which characterize genuine Christian life. It is not possible to sustain, heal and grow without sacrifice, forgiveness, compassion – all portrayed vividly in the life of Jesus. Jesus visualized the Kingdom of God as a time when justice, peace, equality would be lived fully. For these to be present, sacrifice, forgiveness and compassion are the personal characteristics needed.

As a signpost to our exploration in the following chapters, a summary may be helpful. I believe that each marriage is a place whose life is love and, as such, a place where couples encounter God through each other. Each family is a place where the kingdom of God is experienced in wholeness, insofar as justice, peace and equality is lived. This is brought about by sustaining, healing and growing love which in turn is supported by sacrifice, forgiveness and compassion. Thus, in encountering God each moment of their life, the love that couples have is their daily prayer. Their prayer is their love for each other, a love which is truly human in its sustaining, healing and growth and nurtured by the Christian virtues of sacrifice, forgiveness and compassion.

This Part, as its title indicates, is concerned with marriage. I hope that readers who are not married will nevertheless find much here that is relevant to them in their own situations, but I have neither the space nor the particular experience to spell out here how other states of life may equally embody God's calling and gift of love.

One

God in everyday marriage

The most common prayer that the ordinary Christian learns is the 'Our Father', and, coming as it does from the mouth of Jesus himself, it is perhaps the most important prayer we know. This prayer emerges from Jesus' relationship with his Father, and without this fuelling energy the prayer would be meaningless.

Although the New Testament is packed with powerful sayings, few carry such dynamic meaning as these:

> My dear people,
> Let us love one another
> Since love comes from God
> and everyone who loves is begotten by God and knows God.
> Anyone who fails to love can never have known God
> because God is Love.
> (1 John 4:7–8)

> My dear people,
> Since God has loved us so much
> We too should love one another.
> No one has ever seen God;
> but as long as we love one another
> God will live in us
> and his love will be complete in us.
> (1 John 4:11–12)

God is love
and anyone who lives in love lives in God
and God lives in him.
(1 John 4:16)

It is not surprising that so many people have abandoned going to church because the central prayer of their life, expressed in relationship with those they love, has never been accorded a high priority by church leaders. In fact, this is not surprising. It is much easier to string words together, to have a long list of different prayers for different occasions, than to pay attention to loving.

Love is so often connected with feelings and emotions, the part of the personality that has often been underrated compared with reason and will. In a male-dominated world, feelings and emotions have been associated with women, and the ways they are expressed, such as tears, sympathy, dramatic gestures, have been dismissed as unworthy of the stoicism men should demonstrate.

But Scripture and our experience make it very clear that human love is the most basic way to find and live the life of God. In loving we do not recite words, do not genuflect, nor cross ourselves. The central element of love is to become aware of another person whose good we pursue. We do not have to fall in love or be moved in order to express love; we have to be in a relationship with another person which can span minutes or a lifetime.

Prayer doesn't consist just of saying prayers but of a loving awareness of the depth and the creative power in life that Christians call 'God'. So long as we love with integrity and authenticity, we are in a state of continuous prayer. In loving we are in direct contact with God, and the neighbour we love becomes Jesus in our life. Loving assumes its own sacramentality. In other words, through loving we meet God in each other every minute of our life.

With this introduction to love and prayer, we can turn to the specific instance of marriage and the family. In the Roman Catholic tradition this relationship is a very special one which has been defined as a sacrament. In the Protestant tradition it has also a higher status of being a 'Holy Estate'. And we should understand that men and women in the state of marriage who have been incorporated through baptism in the life of Jesus Christ, and who are authentically loving each other, are in a continuous state of prayer. The grace of the sacrament is this well of love flowing from one spouse to the other in and through their love of each other. For those not incorporated in

17

Christianity through baptism, the same principle applies. Prayer is the awareness of God, and marital love is an implicit life of prayer for the non-believer. The state of marriage is given by God to be the place where the spouses' love is given and received, and by giving and receiving love they become part of the activity of God.

The events of the day become the liturgy of the domestic church. As the couple rise, wash, dress, have breakfast, go to work, take the children to school, clean the house, prepare food, return in the evening, eat together, discuss things, go to bed, make love, they are participating in their domestic church whose liturgy is these events. Whenever the couple are relating to each other and their children, they are in a state of prayer.

The Second Vatican Council refers to the domestic church:

> For from the wedlock of Christians there comes the family,
> in which new citizens of human society are born. By the
> grace of the Holy Spirit received in Baptism, these are made
> children of God, thus perpetuating the People of God
> through the centuries. The family is, so to speak, the
> Domestic Church.

The concept of the domestic church is new to many people. In fact, the theology of marriage in all the Christian churches is hardly understood at all, and yet we have arrived at a point in which the secular seeking of love and the theological orientation of love in marriage are coming together.

For the majority of human beings, not just for Christians, married love is the means of salvation, the way people share in God's activity. The daily human encounters of love become the channel of communicating with God through Jesus Christ. The domestic church is the home where the couple celebrate God's presence through each other and their children. This celebration occurs every day, every minute of the day, and then the family come together to worship in the midst of the community in the local church on Sunday. The concept of the domestic church becomes a bridge between the private celebration of the presence of God and that of the community.

In this chapter a great deal has been said about love as the daily prayer of the married. The reader may be wondering about the nature of love. Not only is love an extremely complex term, but it has developed over the centuries. The subsequent chapters will try to show what contemporary love in marriage implies.

Reflection

- If 'married love becomes the means of salvation of the majority of human beings', how should that affect our attitude to married people who are not Christians and to their marriages?
  e.g. – how we value them?
    – how we do what we can to give appropriate support to their marriages?
    – our willingness to be inspired and helped by their good example?
- 'The events of the day become the liturgy of the domestic church.' Are there events in your own family which make you gratefully aware of God's loving care?

TWO

Everyday marriage and love

How is love expressed in contemporary marriage? There is no definition of love in relationships, which accounts for the rich array of the experience. Millions of words have been written about how love affects men and women, and increasingly people of the same sex. In the Sonnets of Shakespeare we find a vast collection of pearls on love, as, for example, in Sonnet 116:

> Let me not to the marriage of true minds
> Admit impediments; love is not love
> Which alters when it alteration finds,
> Or bends with the remover to remove.
> Oh no, it is an ever-fixèd mark
> That looks on tempests and is never shaken;
> It is the star to every wandering bark,
> Whose worth's unknown although his height be taken.
> Love's not Time's fool, though rosy lips and cheeks
> Within his bending sickle's compass come;
> Love alters not with his brief hours and weeks
> But bears it out even to the edge of doom.
> If this be error and upon me proved,
> I never writ, nor no man ever loved.

In this description, love is something powerful and constant which envelops two human beings. This is the falling-in-love stage in which the beloved appears handsome, faultless and desirable. This is the time when the twosome want to be together as much and as long as possible, when being together is a heavenly experience as they discover the details about each other. Faults are minimized and conflict is soon resolved. There is a desire for happiness and instant joy. This period lasts for months, and it is followed by the wish to marry, or maybe in these days to cohabit. But on what terms does love endure after this initial flush of exuberance?

Traditionally marriage has been a state in which the man and woman had separate and different roles to play. The husband was considered to be the provider. He went out to work, and the family relied on his income for its survival. Working was associated with other significant activities. The husband was the head of the family. It was he who took the main decisions and was responsible for order in the household. It was the husband who was the ambassador of the family to the outside world. His word was taken seriously, backed as it was by economic power.

The woman was not expected to work outside the home, but to stay at home and organize it. She was the childbearer and rearer, and responsible for the emotional life of the family. It was she who smoothed things between the members of the household, and was constantly available to meet the needs of the members of the family, particularly those of the husband.

All this has changed. Women are now working in large numbers and supporting their families. In some instances the woman becomes the chief provider. Economic considerations have forced both partners to be earners, and this means that women are not totally dependent on their husbands. A partial explanation for this is over a hundred years of education for women which has opened up many opportunities.

This educational advance and the economic changes have affected the relationship between the couple. Gone is the traditional authoritarian position of the husband as head of the household. People increasingly expect a dialogue between equals, and that the decisions should be made on a basis, not of authority and power, but of mutual agreement and trust. Women are no longer seen as second-class citizens, and the dialogue between the spouses is based on equality.

Women still remain the childbearers, but the size of most families has been greatly reduced, and with modern advances in medicine the majority of pregnancies end in healthy babies. The combination of a smaller family and healthy pregnancies means that the active time

21

spent being pregnant has been greatly reduced, freeing women for other activities. These activities are not limited to housework because husbands are now contributing more than ever to the daily running of the home.

So, whether it be work, actual relationship, dialogue or decision-making, modern marriage has changed from a contract of social requirements which, when backed by mutual faithfulness, rendered the marriage sound and intact. This contract did not mean that loving did not enter the relationship, but it did mean that loving was primarily seen in carrying out social roles.

What is happening now? The marriage relationship is currently being influenced by other factors. Where before social duties and obligations were the background of marriage, now the key to every-thing is a personal relationship of love. How has this come about? As material standards have improved out of all recognition, there has been a subtle transition into the world of feelings, emotions and sexual fulfilment. Love is measured much more by feelings and the expectations of the couple have risen considerably. Women in par-ticular are not prepared to put up with behaviour that would have been acceptable a generation or two ago. In the next few chapters I shall outline in more detail what these expectations are. Couples want to go beyond the falling-in-love stage to loving itself, which is considered a dynamic process that will carry them for the next fifty years of their marriage.

The first phase of marriage is occupied with a continuation of mutual discoveries. The couple learn to rely on each other for their survival. Loving is experienced here as mutual understanding, the exchange of words and actions that give pleasure, the presence of reliability and responsibility, sexual joy, and time spent together. The pleasure of this early phase of marriage is largely taken up in being together. The couple rejoice in each other's presence, render-ing small or big services.

Life is, of course, taken up by work, provision of meals, cleaning the house, shopping, visiting friends. This is the framework within which the couple explore their mutual worlds. What do they like? Dislike? How good are they at communicating with each other? Are they able to apologize when things go wrong? Do they go into a huff when upset? Can they cope with each other's friends and relatives? Do they read accurately the mutual signals of tiredness, irritability, exasperation and, above all, anger? Can they cope with the anger of each other, or are they afraid to quarrel in case they lose their good feelings? These early years are a time to build a mutual awareness of each other, and to learn to overcome their difficulties.

God's creativity reflected in the desire to be parents

With the passage of time the desire to have children usually emerges. This step forward calls for a close examination of both spouses' feelings. Initially a baby involves the mother more than the father, not only because the wife has to carry the baby for nine months, but because caring for the baby may put a stop to her work, confine her to the home, and restrict her life considerably. Is she ready for these changes? Is the husband ready to lose some of the exclusive attention which he has received from his wife? Can he overcome feelings of jealousy for the baby? A baby makes heavy demands on the parents. They have to be prepared to be woken several times during the night, to cope with the tiredness that this brings about and still to remain aware of each other as a couple.

Children undoubtedly bring pleasure to the parents. The baby's smile is a joy, the crawling on the floor, the first tooth, the halting steps, the walking, the arrival of speech, are all milestones of considerable pride to the parents. There is no more exacting and demanding requirement than to bring a life into the world and watch it develop. Soon the child will be asking the meaning of the wonder of its surroundings, and the parents will have the excitement of examining the ordinary things of life afresh from the child's point of view.

Growth in this phase of marriage will require the ability to give the child a lot of time and attention, whilst the personal relationship of the couple grows deeper. Their love for each other is now deepened by the social awareness that they have brought a new life into the world. They become aware of being needed as never before. In the early years of the child's life its survival depends on the vigilance of the parents. They have not only given life to their child but they have to sustain it. There are difficulties associated with this process. For some mothers the world of the baby reduces the frontiers of their life. Changing nappies, feeding, bathing, may become a very small orbit for them. They may long to return to the adult milieu of conversation and challenge.

These mothers long for the husband to return home at night to bring a whiff of adulthood and maturity. The husband may find his wife preoccupied with the baby and himself temporarily at the fringe of his wife's life. It is important during these first five years of life of the child that the couple do not lose their awareness of each other as husband and wife. It is only too easy to be overwhelmed by the baby and to forget that they are a man and woman needing each other's love to be sustained. That is why it is necessary to maintain the good will of relatives and parents which can allow baby-sitting and free time for the couple.

These first five years of married life have been shown by research to be crucial for the survival of the marriage. Not only do a third of all marriage breakdowns occur in these first five years but, at whatever stage a marriage breaks down, the experiences of these early years are crucial.

Later on in the marriage troubled spouses go back to these early years and remember crucial events. Some of them feel that they were not in love when they got married. They had hoped that love would enter their relationship later on and that did not happen. They may harbour resentments about the husband being absent at the time of the birth, being abroad, or having got drunk when the mother and baby returned home. They may remember birthdays being forgotten, or parents treated shabbily by spouses. Times of illness are crucial. Husbands or wives in bed, with partners panicking or not knowing how to provide food, generate resentment which gnaws away inside for years. So love is experienced by the way that care has been shown during these early years.

What about the middle years? These are the two decades from 30 to 50. How does love grow during these years?

Routine is part of prayer

The daily routine of shopping, cooking, cleaning, maintaining the house goes on uninterruptedly. Love is experienced at this level by reliability and sharing of responsibility. The home has to be kept, the food provided, socializing undertaken. In all these events the couple have to rely on each other to perform their respective duties and responsibilities. In this domestic domain problems can arise. Husbands can start reconstructing the kitchen, and the wife finds that two years later the kitchen is still being done. In the meantime the kitchens of several people up and down the street have been attended to. Starting something and not finishing it is a small thing but can make a partner unloved.

In the course of the day punctuality plays a very large part in loving. How often do husbands get ready to go out, only to find that their wives are never ready on time? Wives bitterly complain that husbands rarely arrive on time for the evening meal. The wife may go to a great deal of trouble to cook a nice meal, only to find that it dries up in the oven because the husband is late in leaving work, or he has more than one pint on the way home. Drink may become a source of contention between the spouses, particularly if one of them, especially the wife, has unpleasant childhood memories of a drunken father. The slightest whiff of alcohol on her husband's breath and she goes berserk.

In the home itself tidiness plays an important role for some couples. The husband comes home in the evening and finds it tidy, but fails to show appreciation of how much effort has gone into achieving this. Young children may render any home a pigsty, and the sustained work put in by wives to tidy up may not be appreciated by the husband.

Marital love is sacrificial

The sense of being appreciated for running and maintaining a pleasant home is certainly the background of love in the daily life of many couples during these two decades. They are now getting to know and predict the inner world of each other. The time for new revelation is the response to crisis. In a sense every day has its small crisis which is shared by the couple and with their relatives and friends.

But how they respond to major crises is an occasion for further insights into their personality. How do they take a serious illness? A loss of job? A financial crisis? An affair? Each one of these situations brings out into the open a new range of character traits. An illness is a time to discover disablement, pain, death, and how one copes with each of these situations. Fear, anxiety, depression or stoicism, defiance, trust in God, are all possibilities that emerge. In particular, illness reduces adults to childlike states of dependence and fear. How does the spouse cope with a husband or wife who is a solid, rock-like person one day and a jelly-like frightened child the next? Cancer in particular strikes at the very roots of survival, and when the wife discovers, for example, a lump in her breast there is need for major coping mechanisms to deal with the situation. Every day that the spouses travel by road there is the possibility of an accident, serious or fatal. How someone responds to serious illness is an expression of love.

Also, there is the experience of losing a job, perhaps the key earning job. Losing a job is much more than a loss of income. It is an attack on one's self-esteem, and the response of the spouse is vital. Does the partner make one feel unconditionally lovable, or is appreciation based on what one is worth? Loss of work may make a couple rally to one another or it may produce bitter recrimination.

An affair, which happens in nearly 50 per cent of marriages, can shake the foundations of a marital relationship. An affair can be fleeting, but is often discovered and then there is deep hurt. Even in our sexually permissive society an affair attacks the sense of deep trust that couples have for each other. Nevertheless, the path of forgiveness and reconciliation may deepen a relationship in the aftermath.

Finally, during these two decades the parents of the spouses are likely to get seriously ill or die. During illness the spouse of the sick parent needs support and active help to make visiting possible, and to have a chance to talk about their worries. An even greater sacrifice may be needed when the sick parent or elderly couple must be taken into the marital home and given shelter for perhaps a number of years. There is no doubt that the whole range of crises just described can deepen the bonds between the spouses.

In addition to the daily routine and the serious crises, the couple have to face the challenges of their middle years. With the passage of time they become aware of physical changes. The sense of no longer being young may make husbands and wives anxious about appearance, health and sexual prowess. These factors may be a reason for having an affair.

Amidst this turmoil there may emerge a serene sense of confidence and security of persevering achievement, and the couple may find a new awareness in each other. These are the years when spouses realize that they matter to each other more than their external worth. A deeper sense of love as they appreciate the qualities of loyalty and communication may make them feel they have entered a deeper sense of mutual awareness.

These are also the years when men and women may grow in status. Caring for children and home, and finding responsibility and promotion at work, help them to realize more of their potential. They have greater confidence in themselves, and their self-esteem blossoms. This growth in potential is sometimes recognized at work, by

26

friends and relatives, but it is most important that it is appreciated mutually by the spouses. The spouses grow in the eyes of each other, and the affirmation they receive becomes the single most important source of confidence in their life.

In fact, work and home between them can boost the morale of spouses more than anything else. This affirmation leads the couple to explore new horizons in their life. Growth is not confined to childhood and youth. During the middle years the spouses can expand their horizons, their activities, their wisdom and discover new potential in themselves. If the new potential is realized and appreciated by each other it deepens their love.

As they grow in mutual awareness, the couple have to respond to their children. They do this by models of behaviour, opinions and values, by offering encouragement and affirmation to them, by gently chiding and exhorting, and by generally providing a background of support. The children continue to provide pleasure and joy as they master new challenges, and as they grow in maturity.

When the children have left home

The children in fact act as a cement for the whole family, holding it together and being a source of encouragement for further deepening of the bonds between the partners. Though for some, children's problems and difficulties can be very painful at this time. How parents cope with this can affect their relationship with each other.

Finally the time comes when the children have to leave home. There is retirement from work, and nowadays couples enter two, three or four decades of living together and enjoying each other's company after the children grow up. These decades are very much more available in Western societies and the growth of love during them is little understood. What happens is that the couple can assume a certain basis of mutual love and explore new worlds together. The absence of infirmity can allow them to travel and investigate new possibilities of togetherness. They can rely on each other, and a new phase enters their life as their children marry and their grandchildren arrive.

The deepening of love of the couple over many decades has been outlined in this chapter, but we all know that love thrives on the moments of intimacy which are often physical and sexual as well as being personal and emotional. These are the moments when the bigger plan of love gives way to the moment-to-moment experience of being loved in the way we were loved as children.

Love in childhood was concerned with touching, seeing, hearing mother and father, being in touch with them with words, basking in their pleasure, feeling recognized, wanted and appreciated. All this goes on in adulthood. The special love of adulthood intimacy is described in the next four chapters.

Reflections

- Married life has a transforming quality which contributes to wholeness. This is a great prayer of life in the couple and it is a poignant announcement of the good news in their life.
- Do we appreciate this good news?
- Do we need to reflect in each of our marriages on what we have achieved?

Questions

- In your own experience and that of others you know well, which phases of marriage were/are:
  - most enjoyable?
  - most demanding?
  - more important for helping to make the marriage a personal relationship of love?
  - least expected?
  - least helped?
- What help would you most like couples to receive, that they don't already have, for some of these phases?

Three

Sustaining

The emotional relationship between the spouses depends on a background of several factors. These are availability, caring, communicating, demonstration of affection and resolution of conflict. Each one of these features will be considered in turn, and they form an essential constituent of loving. This loving is often a repetition of childhood experiences now being transacted in adult life. In fact, loving in marriage is the second intimate phase of togetherness, the first being childhood. We transfer to adulthood the moment-to-moment intimacy of childhood.

Availability

We start off with the concept of availability. We began life by having the womb of our mother available for nine months. At the time of birth we first experienced love by forming a bond. This bond of childhood was an experience mediated by sight, sound and touch. We began to recognize the features of our mother within days of birth, and similarly we became familiar with her voice and touch. Between them, sight, sound and touch form the essential link between ourselves and our spouse. This is the essential feature of togetherness. An elementary feature of love is being thus physically together.

There are couples who find it hard to be out of touch with each

29

other, and are in each other's arms constantly. They telephone from work, and they keep in contact with messages of love and concern. But this availability is usually experienced in being together in a room, going for a walk, being in bed or sitting side by side. The availability is intensely physical, and is the basis on which love survives.

Some people find this physical togetherness suffocating, and when there is a combination of a partner who longs for closeness with one who finds it difficult to be close, then there is a great deal of tension. For the one who longs for closeness, finding themselves in the presence of their beloved is a sign of feeling recognized, appreciated and wanted. The physical presence of their partner is a measure of how much they feel wanted.

In ordinary daily life this physical availability can, as I said, present problems when one spouse is not keen on it, but usually a couple have to strike a balance of togetherness and separateness. Separateness is described as having space. Having space is linked with ownership of oneself. Spouses feel that the relationship they have entered gives them access to one another, but not to the extent of being possessed by the other. Freedom to be oneself and to have the right to go about as one pleases has become important for contemporary couples.

Whilst they are aware that togetherness is important, there are situations when one spouse acts in a possessive manner. For example, one meets in counselling situations early in the marriage husbands and wives who take a dislike to their partner's friends and relatives. If the spouse wants to spend time with them, this is resented. Such a partner acts in a jealous or possessive manner, and does not allow their spouse out of their sight. Such possessiveness is not love. It is very unhealthy. It indicates that this spouse is either so insecure that they are frightened to lose their partner to a third party, or find it so difficult to stay alone that they need the physical presence of their husband and wife constantly in attendance.

If one finds oneself experiencing such feelings, it is part of loving to try and overcome them. This is where loving and prayer become linked in an effort to combat the feelings of fear and insecurity. As will be explained in the next chapter, healing consists of facing honestly one's emotions and difficulties, sharing these feelings with one's spouse, and then working together to overcome them. In the case of possessiveness the constant demand for closeness is not an expression of love, but a fear of being alone, or of the pending loss of one's spouse to a third party. These feelings have to be faced, and the spouse allowed their freedom whilst the fears are being conquered.

The difficulties of physical availability arise more often nowadays when the couple are so busy, working such long hours that they do not have time for each other. This physical neglect has emotional repercussions in that the physical absence means that they do not reinforce their love for each other. I regularly meet in counselling situations couples who are so busy during the week that they do not spend a single evening together, and at the weekend they are trying to catch up with the chores of the week, or socializing.

It is imperative in such circumstances to stop and evaluate the situation. I advise such couples that, whatever their individual circumstances, they should make sure that one evening is kept free for themselves in which they share their inner world over a drink or cup of tea or coffee, and remind themselves that they belong to each other.

Modern life has put a premium on physical availability because couples are so busy with their personal lives. Another feature that has to be considered is that spouses can be so occupied with good works that they are out every evening. One evening is taken up with the choir, the next with a prayer meeting, the third visiting the elderly and infirm, the fourth visiting the sick, the fifth can be youth work, and in this way the whole week disappears. Whilst good works have their own validity, being physically available to one's spouse has its own priority.

Enough has been said about physical availability to show that it is a central experience of love. But in the presence of one's spouse there has to be discerning of what mood they are in and responding accurately to that mood. In psychological terms emotional availability is called empathy. Empathy means being in touch with the inner world of one's partner. Are they angry? Frightened? Perplexed? Confused? Worried? Unhappy? Or just quietly contented? Being in touch with the mood of one's spouse is vital if one is to reach them.

Women on the whole are much better at recognizing moods than men, although individual men can be very perspicacious. On the whole the moods that produce problems are not the ones that are bathed in joy or pleasure. It is the negative moods that produce problems, when one's spouse is angry, irritated, unhappy. They can be explosive with their tension, but also go very quiet and not say a word. When asked how they feel, they shrug their shoulders and say that they are all right. They find it difficult to express their feelings.

Here a balance has to be struck between respect for the silence of one's partner with the desire, on the other hand, to reach them and help them to unburden themselves.

Being in touch with the mood of one's spouse means being prepared to experience the pain and agony of their inner world. Apart from not being in tune with the mood of our partner, we may be frightened of being put in a position of listening to and confronting someone in distress. Learning to feel what our spouse feels and yet not being overwhelmed by the contents is a challenge of empathy which takes time to learn.

We start relationships with the desire to be helpful and have the capacity to cheer our partner, whatever the circumstances. This we cannot always do. What we can do is to allow our partner to share their feelings with us and to give them the signals that we have understood their feelings. In this way they are no longer isolated. They feel they have been reached, and the key to empathy is to be reached.

Thus emotional availability is the ability to be in touch with the inner world of our spouse, to make them feel they are not alone, they no longer need to be frightened, and they are not isolated.

Between them, physical and emotional availability constitute twin ingredients of love, and they reflect the first two years of life before we could speak when we felt close to our mother and father. This was a closeness of body and mood, and in an ideal situation we felt close to each other. Couples know when they are close to each other, and this is the experience of feeling in love.

Caring is also God's work

Physical closeness is, of course, present in other situations. We are physically close in a bus, a Tube, a plane, a cinema, in a football stadium. We are physically close whenever we are herded together, but we do not get any special feelings or meaning out of these conditions. They are necessary for us to fulfil whatever purpose we are undertaking. Strangers may be thrown in our lap in the bus or in the Tube, but they do not stimulate any special reaction in us.

Thus physical availability by itself has no great significance for us. Is it familiarity that is the key to feeling significant in the presence of the other? Not so. We meet people regularly as we travel, and we do not want to fling our arms around them. We meet our fellow workers at work regularly (and Part Three of this book tries to show how other kinds of love can find a home in the workplace), but they do not elicit special feelings in us.

When we come to our spouse, he or she does elicit a particular dimension of feelings which we call affection. Their presence gives us feelings of warmth, joy, pleasure, reassurance and meaning. We know we matter because this man or this woman elicits in us feelings of concern. We want to be near them, this we have established. We want to know what is happening to them. What is happening to them is a matter of concern. There are ties of meaning and affection with those we love.

We do not want anything unwelcome to happen to them, and we want to rush to their rescue when they are in distress. This is a reminder of the instincts mothers and fathers have in relation to their children. When a child cries it emits a signal of distress, and we rush to comfort it. Love consists of the awareness that the other person is significant in our life, and their presence elicits signals of concern in us.

These signals of concern lead us to prepare food for them, take care of them when they are ill, comfort them when they are in distress. There is an affective bond between us which emits signals of affection all the time. So when we see them, or when they are away from us, we surround their presence with feelings of concern. We can be curious, fascinated, sexually aroused by *any*body, but we care about *some*body.

Caring is, of course, something we can do professionally. The doctor, the nurse, the social worker, the priest, can all care for their particular group of people. But this caring is a specialized meeting of needs. When caring is linked to love then the very existence of the beloved elicits a state of alertness that someone important in our life is present, and when they are present we want to touch them, convey to them our special regard, loving them, kissing them, making them feel the subject of our concern and affection.

Caring in this way distinguishes physical togetherness from loving presence. But not everyone has the capacity to be involved in this affectionate caring. There are men and women who are cold, frozen, unmoved, unable to show their feelings, to be affectionate or concerned. How do we find ourselves linked in marriage with such people whom psychologists call schizoid? Surely the last thing we want is to be connected with such a person.

Sometimes what happens is that such a cold person overcomes

their withdrawn state in the excitement of courtship. They are carried along by the excitement of falling in love, and in that state they overrule their frozen feelings. When the falling-in-love state subsides and is replaced by loving, their normal cautious, undemonstrative self returns.

Another way of getting attached to an undemonstrative person is due to the experience of a childhood in which we were not shown a great deal of demonstrative love. We did not become accustomed to receive signals of caring and affection. We grew up hungry for affection, but unable to get close to men and women who sent out such signals because the very things we wanted overwhelmed us. So we settled for a relationship in which we got limited demonstration of affection which in fact maintained, in adult life, our childhood state.

When a situation arises in which one of the spouses is undemonstrative or cannot show their feelings of caring, this does not mean that he or she does not care. But if they are married to someone who is hungry for signals of care and affection then difficulties arise. These difficulties are compounded when the hungry person seeks affection outside the marriage. When these difficulties are present they have to be faced honestly. The spouse who wants evidence of affection needs to make his/her feelings known to his/her partner, and he/she must make every effort to overcome inertia with feelings.

Success is achieved with little beginnings, when some form of affirmation is made. When it is made, it is essential for the spouse to acknowledge it. In this way encouragement is given and even more effort is put into being demonstrative and affirmative.

Difficulties are compounded when one spouse is both a loner and undemonstrative, and is married to someone who is hungry for togetherness and demonstration of affection. These are the problems that are met in counselling, but they are represented in ordinary marriages. A common combination is the marriage of the extrovert with the introvert, that is to say, a marriage in which one spouse is demonstrative and expressive, and the other reticent and receptive. But the most common combination is the one in which two partners are equal in concern for each other.

So far we have shown that love begins at the level of physical and emotional availability which means a combination of togetherness and empathy. We move on to strong concern for each other, in which the relationship becomes special by the presence of affectionate bonds with each other, and to communicating this special quality of feeling.

Communication

The gift of language is the most precious capacity we have as human beings, and it differentiates us from animals. Men and women can spend time together, be physically close, and be aware of each other as special, but in the end they need to talk to each other.

Women are much better at talking than men. They can get hold of small items of information and enlarge them into crucial significance. When telephoning between members of the family, mothers and daughters have the capacity to exchange a whole range of interesting topics, whilst the father cuts the conversation into what he considers essentials and the whole exchange comes to a halt in a minute.

Communicating is an essential part of love. When spouses are talking to each other, each item of information is part of the identity of the talker, and it conveys a significant message about the inner world. It will not do just to hear the words that are uttered. We need to appreciate their mood, their relevance to the relationship, requests for action, exchange of relevant information. Very often when we are talking we are revealing our most inner feelings and ideas. How we are received matters enormously to us.

So what have we learned about listening to each other? Love is intimately connected with listening. We have to hear the message of our spouse, not just words or reasoning, but also the feelings that accompany the words. A combination of listening with uninterrupted care may mean that we are the first person who has ever listened carefully to what they have to say. At the end of each day when spouses have had to keep their mouths shut in umpteen situations it is refreshing to have an opportunity to pour out their feelings and ideas.

Listeners are often overwhelmed by the feeling that they have personally to put right all the injustices perpetrated on their spouses during the day. 'Why are you telling me all this? What can I do?' The point is not that there is an expectation to put right some injustice. What is needed is to be listened to so that the matter can be ventilated, feelings expressed and a sense of justice reached in the haven of home. In this way the next day can be faced.

Listening has to be non-judgemental. Spouses are afraid to open their mouth because they expect to be criticized. Loving in listening means that one is prepared to receive the inner world of one's spouse. This reception is not there to titillate our curiosity or to be voyeuristic. The inner world of our partner is not there to amuse us or to make us feel righteous by comparison. We are there to receive in a non-judgemental way the thoughts and actions of our partner. We are not asked to judge or to pass sentence. In this way we generate trust.

Sometimes people ask their partner to remain always frank with them, to tell them everything that concerns them both. When the partner does tell everything, he/she finds that their spouse cannot cope with the truth. The whole truth is too much for them. In this situation we must assess our partner carefully and reveal to them what they are capable of coping with. Frankness is still required, but this frankness has to be tempered with the knowledge that some truths are so unpalatable that they have to be digested in small morsels. Nevertheless, the general policy is always to try and pursue the truth even if it is delivered in small portions.

The difficulty in always telling the truth is the fear that some of our actions may elicit the anger of our partner. The child is afraid of displeasing the parent, and we are afraid of displeasing those we love. A certain amount of tension may be inevitable, but, if we live in the certainty of being loved, reconciliation invariably takes place.

So whether we are the person who is communicating or the person who is listening, when we exchange information we are revealing our soul to each other and become the recipients of each other's inner world. All of these exchanges are moments of loving.

Affirmation

I said just now that our listening should be non-judgemental. If we listen to an ordinary conversation between members of a family, we find that the contents are peppered with remarks: 'That was a stupid thing to do'. 'You are a fool.' 'Of course, I am not surprised, I always told you you were stupid.' 'How many times have I told you to listen to me? You can't be left a moment by yourself and you make a mess of things.'

These remarks are putting down some member of the family, often the spouse. If the spouse has come from a background where he/she has been denigrated, then the continuation of this in the marriage will not come as a surprise. When they are not accustomed to such humiliation, then they get angry and rebel.

Children need constant affirmation when they are growing up. We praise them continuously. 'Good girl this, and good girl that . . . Well done, my boy . . . That's marvellous . . .' We are praising our children because we realize that praise is the basis of learning to do things correctly. Praise builds confidence and self-esteem.

We need praise no less as adults. We need to be constantly thanking our partner, showing them appreciation and acknowledging their worth. Very often what happens in adult relationships is that we stay silent when things go well, and we criticize when things go wrong. What we forget is that someone who has made a mistake carries his or her own sense of guilt inside.

They know they have acted stupidly. We do not need to compound their distress. What is needed is to alleviate it. In fact, the policy in love should be to keep silent when things go wrong and raise the roof in praise when things go right. This is the way of building confidence in each other, and ensuring that on average more success will follow.

Mention has already been made several times of women's emancipation in the current social situation. This is very important, and it has played a part in the domestic scene. In the past women may not always have been brutalized physically but they were often humiliated, being put down by their husbands. In particular, this would happen when a wife insisted on having her way on something important in the home. If the husband did not want to go along with it and had no arguments to counter her case, he might finish up by saying 'The trouble with you is that you are mad. Only mad people think as you do.'

This attitude gradually undermines confidence, the woman becomes depressed and turns to the doctor for help. The husband seizes this recourse to medical help as further evidence of her madness, 'If you are not careful, my girl, I will have to lock you up.' The mental hospital was the ultimate threat of husbands.

I see scores of wives who come to me battered psychologically by husbands who will insist that their wives are in the wrong. Women's emancipation has meant that millions of women are standing up for themselves, and not allowing their husbands to get the better of them.

But affirmation is not confined to being positive towards one's spouse. It means also demonstrating affection to them, telling them that you love them. Demonstration of affection is often associated with sexual overtures, especially in bed, but women in particular are keen to experience affection in non-sexual situations.

Couples may sit side by side and embrace, whisper sweet nothings in each other's ears. This is a reminder of the affection of childhood when we loved to be picked up and embraced in a non-sexual way. There is plenty of room for both sexual and non-sexual demonstration of affection, and this is a key way to express love.

Along the road of sustaining I have mentioned physical and emotional availability, caring, communication and affirmation. I will finish up by saying something about reconciliation.

Reconciliation

The loving relationship of intimacy is particularly vulnerable. When we do not care about people they can annoy us, irritate us, but they do not hurt us. When the person who crosses us is our spouse then we are hurt, our world is temporarily without the sun. People who love one another may have to have arguments, and even quarrels, but they do not want these distractions to their love.

Nevertheless we get angry with each other and our relationship ruptures from time to time. These arguments can be extremely painful, but often what the argument is about is something sacred. Spouses quarrel about aspects of themselves, their beliefs and feelings, their actions, which they consider important.

Quarrels are not about scoring points over each other. The pain of a quarrel is about proclaiming to one's spouse that something vital has been touched, something which is precious to the identity of the spouse. It is the central core of the truth that we have to get hold of and treat with great care and respect in the future.

But that is not how many quarrels proceed. Often when a quarrel begins it is a bitter battle to the end. When anger flies about, spouses' anxiety rises, and defence mechanisms are brought into action. These defences are powerful material. Spouses will protect themselves by rationalizing, denial, projection and paranoid feelings. Instead of listening, they will jump to conclusions. Instead of admitting they are wrong, they will persist to the end that they are right. They will flout the truth in the face of convincing evidence. They will call each other names. They will bring into the current

38

quarrel all the accumulated grievances of the past, and for good measure add the faults of each other's parents. A quarrel will thus become a raw exchange of anger, and hide from each other the central issue of the conflict.

It is worthwhile remembering that in each quarrel there is a central issue, sometimes more than one, which is being defended by the hurt individual. It is vital that this truth be discovered and learned so that it can be respected in the future. Serious quarrels are about sacred truths which have been trampled upon. The sooner one learns the truth and acknowledges it in the midst of all the pain, then the fight can be over.

So I conclude this chapter by summarizing that in sustaining we are concerned in maintaining the moment to moment relationship of the couple in and through love. This sustaining is based on physical and emotional availability, caring, communication, affirmation and demonstration of affection and reconciliation. Each moment has its aspects of drama, its difficulties, and there is plenty of sacrifice required to overcome the problematic situations.

Questions
- In your experience of marriage, which of the five elements in sustaining it mentioned above have been particularly fruitful?
- Which have been most difficult?
- What could have made those easier?
- Could you discuss with your spouse which of them need to be worked on particularly at present?
- How can prayer or reflection together on these elements help a couple to foster, and appreciate, the depth and goodness of their relationship and to overcome its difficulties?
- By appreciating these elements in the marriages of others, are you better able to appreciate and perhaps sometimes help their relationships?

Prayer-notes
Experience Which of your experiences of sustaining in marriage do you value most?

Pointers-to-depth
> You, Lord, are all I have,
>   and you give me all I need;
>   my future is in your hands.

How wonderful are your gifts to me;
  how good they are!

I am always aware of the Lord's presence;
  he is near, and nothing can shake me.

And so I am thankful and glad,
  and I feel completely secure,
because you protect me from the power of death,
  and the one you love you will not
  abandon to the world of the dead.

You will show me the path that leads to life;
  your presence fills me with joy
  and brings me pleasure for ever.
(Psalm 16, Good News Bible)

Response 'He/she is near, and nothing can shake me.' What more could you do to create that feeling in your spouse?

Four

Healing

In the depths of interaction between spouses they will come across not only the strengths and good points in each other's character, but also the weaknesses and the failings. In the past it may have been considered that a successful marriage was one in which the husband earned money for the support of the family, while the wife looked after the children and home adequately, and in which there was no heavy drinking, gambling or violence. Failure to earn enough to live on, heavy drinking, gambling or violence are still a source of trouble in many marriages today. But for a marriage to be seen as successful today, more is expected. The emotional interaction of the couple has become a major concern to them to a far greater extent than in the past, and defects in this area undoubtedly make a major contribution to marriage difficulties, and their handling is the challenge facing many modern marriages. In this chapter I shall outline the main problems and ways to handle them.

In the past when a defect in the personality or in the character was found, the bearer was blamed for it. He/she was held responsible for it and expected to correct it. It was their fault, and they were bidden by fear or punishment to change their behaviour. Nowadays this attitude is still present in some quarters, but a more sympathetic and effective approach is to try and understand the defect as a difficulty which arises as part of the childhood experience of the individual or their genetic make-up.

This interpretation is seen by some as a soft one which offers an excuse, the carrot rather than the stick. The point to remember is that in this new way of looking at things the person still has the obligation to change, but allowance is made for change being slow and difficult, and much more is achieved with help and encouragement rather than moaning and criticizing. As we deal with the broad categories of problems, we shall see that a combination of the desire to change and help from the spouse is the best way forward.

Feeling unloved and unwanted

A great deal of our personality is bestowed upon us by our parents. Over the last hundred years much progress has been made in preventing, curing or correcting many of the gross physical defects caused in the past by such problems as malnutrition or polio, in many countries of the world. And serious attention has been given, with some success, to helping to overcome mental handicaps.

What has been harder to overcome is the series of emotional wounds which are acquired in the presence of inadequate parenting in the first intimate experience of childhood.

These defects reappear in the second intimate experience of love, in marriage, where feeling unlovable and unwanted may permeate the whole personality. The detailed explanation of how these states come about belongs in the textbooks of psychology. Here we are concerned with their effect on the relationship between spouses.

The first step is *to identify and respect the wound in the individual*. It makes a lot of difference if the spouse is labelled as 'attention seeking' which is seen as childishly drawing attention to oneself, or whether the hunger for love is correctly identified and respected.

There is still a prevailing notion that grown-up men and women do not need attention, only children require that. This is an entirely wrong way of looking at things. Saying to your spouse 'All you think of is yourself' is not very helpful when in fact the partner has not developed sufficiently emotionally to be confident about themselves, and to be free to be concerned about others. It is a fact that their development has left them emotionally at a very early stage of development. Making them feel guilty about it does not help. It aggravates the problem in that the person now feels unloved and guilty for needing love. The loving thing to do is to recognize that one's partner is handicapped emotionally, and to try to give them the sort of

42

experience that will help them to grow in the feelings of being loved and wanted. This is easier said than done.

In order to understand the complexity of the situation we have to delve back into childhood. By the time of five or so the child has the beginnings of feeling unconditionally loved, that is to say, they feel loved because they exist, not because they have earned their love.

It is with entry into school that the second experience of feeling loved is learned. Now attention is received for results achieved. The school is the beginning of a lifetime of rewards for things done well. So the person who is short of unconditional love will put all their efforts into feeling wanted and appreciated on the basis of their achievements.

Thus you may have men or women who are greatly gifted in talents of business, intellectual probity; they use their skills to draw attention to themselves. Such men and women depend for their good feelings on the results they attain at work. But back at home and away from the world of attainment, they feel flat, unwanted and unloved. They seek attention like children. They will look at the size of food put on their plate and they want the biggest share. They will tell their children to remain silent until it is their turn to speak, but they themselves will hog the conversation. They will persistently ask their spouse whether they love them, and no sooner have they heard that they are loved, they want to hear it again. It is not that they are deaf, but their capacity to register good feelings and, even more important, to retain them, is limited. They want to be told something good about themselves every day, and if possible every minute.

How does one respond to such a needy person? As with all emotional wounds, spouses try to be sympathetic initially, and then their goodwill fades, they become discouraged, and finally they give up trying. The first thing to recognize is that when you are dealing with an emotional wound the healing is a long haul and it takes time to repair the wound. The wounded individual lost their chance of feeling loved at the critical phase during the development of their life when they should have been given the appropriate signals. When critical moments are passed in human development, repairing the damage is possible but much greater effort, which is sustained over time, is required.

So the deprived husband or wife needs extra attention given at regular intervals. We do not complain when we have to cook afresh every day to provide food. We do not think that feeding once a week is enough, and so the person who feels unloved and unwanted wants to hear that they matter at regular intervals. They want to learn for the first time about unconditional love.

The wife or husband who recognizes the signs of a wounded spouse can exchange them for another person through divorce, or they can persevere in loving them in such a way that healing takes place. The spouse can, at regular intervals, tell the deprived partner that they love them. They can give them special attention when the occasion arises. Such deprived individuals turn to small treats to compensate for their lack of love. Whether it is food, clothes, cars, they resort to material things to make up for their sense of loss. All this should be seen as compensation and not as 'greed' or 'selfishness'. This is not a question of indulging themselves. Indulgence means having things in surfeit.

Such deprived men and women may have a surfeit of material things, but not of love; the material things are used instead of love. That is why such a person may appear mean. Money is an emotional commodity. It is the tangible way of filling up the inner sense of emptiness. Money is used to give a sense of fullness.

All this has to be recognized by the family, indeed, by society as a whole. Some people refuse to look at deprivation in this way on the basis that psychologists make excuses for everybody, and it is much better if men and women acknowledged their wounds as badness and sin, and seek repentance from the Lord. Fundamental Christianity is attractive for some because everything is seen in terms of black and white. For them the person who feels unlovable and unwanted is in need not of love but of repentance.

The trouble with this approach is that if the wound is not recognized as a psychological one and handled psychologically we impose on wounded men and women the injustice of denying their problems and make them feel guilty as if their wounds were their fault. Sin is the direct challenge of God over a particular matter in which the bad is deliberately chosen over the good. In previous times a sin was considered to have taken place when something bad was committed, and there was full freedom and consent in the individual to commit the sin. The trouble with emotionally wounded people is that they are not free agents in their actions.

And so when it comes to feeling unlovable and unwanted, men and women crave for attention, or alternatively behave as if they were self-sufficient, care only for work, which is their sole source of satisfaction, and do not worry whether anybody loves them. This defence is the attempt to put a brave face on their wound. As children they learned to cope without attention, and so they will now as adults sail through life without asking anyone for any favours.

These well-guarded men and women appear to be strong, need little, work hard, very hard, and ignore the emotional aspect. But such an approach to life has a high price to pay. They are lonely and isolated, and although they scorn attention, they have a need for it.

With such well-defended people patience is needed to break through their defences and give them attention and care without making them feel humiliated.

The unloved form an army of men and women who are littered all over society. No social class is immune from these emotional wounds, and healing is a long-term process of giving them in adult life a second chance to experience the love they did not have the first time round in their childhood.

Insecurity

Another wound which is frequently found in men and women is insecurity. What is meant by insecurity? There is first of all physical insecurity which is the fear of being alone. Some men and women hate being alone, left in the home by themselves. They want their partner to be beside them. They do not necessarily mind what their partner does. They can be asleep, or in another part of the house, provided they are within call. Many people find sleeping alone terrifying. They may have to do it, but they do not like it at all. Emotional insecurity is really linked with self-esteem and confidence. Both of them are lacking, and the insecure person feels that he/she will be easily dispossessed. They are afraid that people will find out they are no good and reveal their shallowness. They are afraid of losing their jobs or losing their husband or wife to someone else.

Such people are often jealous and possessive. A jealous person will fear that their spouse will find someone else more attractive. The partner of the insecure person learns to be cautious, not to give a look or a glance which will appear to favour someone else. He/she will learn to be careful with whom they talk, and if they should allow themselves to have an affair the very foundations of the insecure partner's life may be shaken. The jealous partner is convinced that he/she has lost their partner for good. He/she will wear out their partner with questions about the affair, and insist on knowing every detail and comparing it with their own functioning. In his or her own thoughts the jealous person will always come out worse in such a comparison, and nothing will reassure them. The erring partner may be kept awake until the early hours of the morning answering questions, and the jealous person may never be satisfied with the answers. He or she will allow no detail to be passed over; no explanation will be good enough. There is a painful period ahead for both parties until the anxieties of the insecure spouse subside.

Jealousy is one source of torment for their spouse; possessiveness is another. They need to keep their partner close by and under surveillance most of the time. They cannot stay alone, and they are overwhelmed with the fear that, once out of sight, the spouse will never return. So a possessive person restricts, or attempts to restrict, the freedom of their partner. They are discouraged from meeting their friends or relatives. They are encouraged to stay close by the insecure spouse, to keep them company and to go out only with them. In this way they become lonely and isolated.

Jealousy and possessiveness are the twin monsters of insecurity. How do the partners respond to these qualities? Here, as elsewhere with personal wounds, they have to be frankly faced. It is important that the spouse does not begin to act as a victim. It is vital that the jealous person acknowledges their fears and does not hang on to some justifying explanation that their partner is unreliable, sex-mad, disloyal, and their fears are justified. Of course, occasionally they are justified in their fears, but in the overwhelming majority of situations the spouse has not given any justification for the jealousy or the possessiveness. The jealous person has to face their fears of being abandoned, as they may have been in their childhood. The sense of abandonment is at the bottom of these feelings, leading to massive insecurity.

Once the irrationality of the fears has been acknowledged, the partner must, of course, try to do everything in their power not to feed the insecurity. At the same time the insecure person must be encouraged to learn to feel more secure. Every time their partner goes out of sight they have to be encouraged to relax and feel safe on their own. In this way they can learn to spend longer and longer periods on their own.

When their spouse casts an eye on somebody else, the insecure person should be encouraged to express their fears and recognize how irrational they are. This is another way of unlearning the pattern of jealousy and beginning to feel more secure.

Insecurity and jealousy can destroy a relationship and once it is recognized it must not be allowed to proceed unchecked, otherwise it assumes monstrous proportions of fear, doubt and mistrust.

Paranoid reactions

The paranoid personality emerges out of the insecure one. The paranoid person feels threatened by other people who are experienced as hostile and malevolent. They see no accident in their mishaps. They all have the mark of someone 'out there' who perpetrated them. The paranoid person is suspicious, and expects malevolence from every quarter of life. Everyone is against them, and they have to protect themselves from the real and imaginary onslaughts which they receive at regular intervals.

Inevitably the paranoid person is critical of others, who they suspect are up to no good. Paranoid people are hard on themselves and hard on everybody else. They criticize everybody and everything, and their attitude is pessimistic. They do not expect good tidings from anyone.

Most of the time the hostile world is contained and not acted upon, but sometimes it breaks the boundaries of rationality, and then it becomes an illness. Normally paranoid people simply expect to be attacked, and they are, of course, most suspicious of their relatives and spouse. They get angry easily and lose their temper at the slightest provocation. These persistently angry, hot-tempered and unhappy men and women can cause havoc in their families.

They are always seeking new friends, hoping to free themselves from the world of isolation and desolation in which they put themselves. The new friend is welcomed and treated with enthusiasm, as if at last the right person in their life has been found. But soon the new friend disappoints, as everyone before has done, and they too join the long list of a hostile world.

The paranoid person is particularly suspicious of authority, and everyone in authority is part of the system of 'them' who are out to cheat, defraud, exploit, particularly the poor. The world of 'them' and 'us' comes easily to the paranoid person. The family, and particularly the spouse, become part of the great citadel that the paranoid person has to defend against the wicked outside world.

The paranoid person is always a victim of others and, of course, of the 'system'. The system is the government of the day, the boss, the church, any institution, and they all combine to strike down the poor, and the paranoid person is constantly poor compared to others. The home becomes the source of salvation. In the home the spouse and the children are expected to take their side and form a solid block against the 'enemy'.

Paranoid people are often over-sensitive, that is to say, they are easily upset when criticized. For them criticism is not an exchange of truth, a dialogue between two people who are eager to find the truth. Criticism is always interpreted as an attack, and an unjustified one at that. The over-sensitive person does not have to be criticized to take umbrage. Anything which is not actively complimentary can be interpreted as an attack.

If the spouse or the children do not agree with the paranoid partner they too are accused of betrayal and treachery. Loyalty is only interpreted in terms of agreement with his/her views. There is no room for the truth. The truth is what the paranoid person believes it to be.

How does one respond to the paranoid person? With great difficulty. Underneath the paranoia lies the feeling of deep injustice and that of insecurity. There is such a deep hurt of rejection that no one can do justice to the wounded self. Deep, deep inside the person is a sense of feeling let down and betrayed by those he/she needed to trust. The betrayal is often by one or both parents who were critical instead of loving, half-hearted instead of being supportive, judgemental instead of compassionate or caring.

The paranoid person cannot always face the truth or the details of their behaviour. They simply run away from the implications of what they say or do. At the centre of their psyche lies a deep wound of mistrust. They expect to be let down. They provoke people to let them down so that they can confirm their suspicions.

Initially a spouse faced with a paranoid person may have to be careful about what is said. Such a person cannot be confronted with the truth. What they lack is a sense of fairness and justice. They were let down so often in the past that they must not be let down again. When they are promised, something has to be delivered. Trust must be rebuilt little by little. That means that the spouse and the family must be trustworthy. Slowly the paranoid person learns that human beings can be trusted, and they are not always letting us down.

As with all human wounds, the first step is not to argue on rational grounds. It is no use saying to the paranoid person 'You are wrong. Life is not like that.' They will not believe you. Their experience of life is different from yours. What they have to see little by little is that their interpretation is unique to them and reflects their own experience. Their experience is valid, but it does not reflect everybody else's. The paranoid person must be helped to see that there are other possibilities. A combination of kindness, reliability and trustworthiness slowly shifts the experience of the paranoid person from permanent mistrust to gradual trust. The challenge is enormous, and it takes many years of patient understanding for change to take place.

There are many people who say that modern marriages are based on selfishness. If we take healing seriously, the sustained efforts to overcome the wounds of the spouse are some of the most sacrificial efforts that can be effected. When wounds are healed, something of the healing nature of God is revealed.

Anxiety and phobias

All the personality traits described so far probably arise from disturbances in the upbringing of the individual. There are also conditions which are genetically determined, and one of the most common is anxiety. Anxiety is a state of apprehension in which the man or woman feels apprehensive, right through to fearful, about everything that surrounds their life. These fears are often a reminder of those that prevailed in childhood. Thus the dark, being alone, facing a problem or a difficulty, are all accompanied by anxiety.

Living with an anxious spouse means that there is always a certain amount of tension in the household. Anxiety surrounds any incidence of ill health, which is always interpreted as life-threatening. Everything is experienced with insecurity. The job held is constantly under threat, the late arrival from work is associated with an accident, ill luck shadows activities, and the person lives in a turmoil of concern. This general anxiety can be very debilitating, and, whilst every sympathy should be given to the sufferer, they should not be pandered to. We now have means of helping anxious people, and when the anxiety is high they should be resorted to.

Anxiety can take specific forms, such as problems in which the anxious person is overwhelmed with fear in particular situations. Agoraphobia is fear of open spaces. Claustrophobia is fear of closed spaces, and there are other fears, such as of travelling in aeroplanes, or of heights. All these fears are called phobias, and desensitizing of these fears can be achieved.

Another form of anxiety is to be found in obsessional states, in

49

which the individual is compelled to repeat thoughts, words or actions, or else they are overwhelmed by anxiety. Common obsessions are washing rituals. Every time a knob of the door is touched the individual has to wash their hands to get rid of the imagined germs which were picked up. Thus, washing is not a simple affair. The washing has to be repeated several times, and in the end sufferers spend hours at their ablutions.

Spouses married to partners with obsessions get acclimatized to their minor forms. These minor forms include coming downstairs and checking whether the doors have been locked; returning home to check whether the gas or electricity has been switched off. All these can be lived with, but more severe forms need treatment.

Depression

Depression is one of the most common forms of disability in society. Millions of men and women are sufferers.

In the depressed state the man or woman feels in low spirits, has little energy or drive, is not enthusiastic about anything, is worried and apprehensive and expects dreadful things to happen. Their sleep suffers, their appetite is poor, and their sexual drive wanes. This is the severe form which undoubtedly needs treatment, but less severe forms are common when individuals withdraw into themselves, feel low in spirits, find it difficult to cheer up, and have a despondent outlook on life.

These minor forms are very common, and spouses have to live with spells of withdrawal and despondency in their partners. In these circumstances patience, activation, cheering up and toleration are all needed. When the depression recurs, as it is likely to do, this can be a very severe and taxing burden on the non-depressed partner, and it requires a great deal of loving. These are the days when every moment is a living prayer of patience and toleration.

Conclusion

I have mentioned already, but it is worth repeating, that modern marriage offers a unique opportunity to reactivate, in the intimacy of the relationship, the wounds inflicted in the personality the first time round in the intimacy of the parent–child relationship. The second intimacy of marriage offers an opportunity for healing which is a unique occasion for love and prayer. This healing takes time and offers a very good reason for the durability of marriage. Healing is a modern expression of love, and we have yet to explore the range and possibilities of this particular grace.

The whole Christian faith is about healing wounds and completing the image of God in each one of us. Marriage offers a tremendous chance for this healing to take place, and the insights of psychology have opened a new dimension of love in marriage.

Reflection
'Healing is a modern expression of love, and we have yet to explore the range and possibilities of this particular grace.'

Reflect on your own experience of healing in marriage as 'a modern expression of love':

- What have you valued most in that experience?
- Where would you have valued more exploration?
- How does your reflection help you appreciate the grace of healing in marriage?
- When people in your locality want some help with such healing, where can they turn to?
- Does your church offer help? If not, should it? If so, to whom?

Prayer-notes
Experience In all our deepest relationships we become aware of defects in our emotional interactions. In the loving, patient healing of those, have you seen glimpses of the healing work of God helping us towards human wholeness?

Pointers-to-depth Recall some of the relationships that Jesus tried to heal in the gospels, because the Spirit of God was in him.

Response Which of the emotional wounds discussed here is of particular relevance to your relationship? What could you do to heal the wound, however gradually and patiently?

Five

Growth

The intimate love of the couple has so far been described in the moment-to-moment experience of sustaining and the more leisurely unfolding of healing.

There is a third dimension, not so well understood as either of these, which comprises the process of growth. As the couple spend several decades together they invariably change. This change is a complex process of the physical, the social, and the emotional. We only understand it in parts, but within it the love–prayer dimension is to be found.

Physical

Marriage often starts in the twenties, and the fresh, attractive appearance of the couple is a strong erotic basis for the physical encounter. The physical shape remains the same for long periods at a time, but gradually the grey hair appears, weight is added, and the smoothness of the skin fades. At about the age of 50 the wife has her menopause, with the end of childbearing, but not the end of sexual activity. Nevertheless, the link between appearance and sex continues through all the decades and many a marital breakdown has occurred because of the wish to exchange a spouse for a younger-looking one. Love is needed to remain faithful to changing appearances.

52

Another aspect of love is the care given at times of sickness. Transient illness in the prime of life demands attention, but it is in the prolonged care when infirmity appears with age that special loving is needed.

Then there is always death to face, at whatever age. Facing death makes sharp demands on composure, tenacity and faith. With the certainty of death hanging over a spouse the challenge is to help them live life to the full. Of course, impending death raises feelings of loss and how one is going to cope without one's beloved. Even a strong faith does not diminish the anguish of loss, which is primarily physical. After death there is grieving, which is the pain of the active loss of physical contact. In terms of physical availability, the person is no longer present. What happens, however, is that the memories of the deceased gradually assemble in those living. These memories are internalized in the spouse who has their deceased living inside them. In this way the acute grieving gives way over time to a tranquillity of possessing the lost one.

Social

In the field of social change the most obvious one is upward and downward social mobility. In upward social mobility success at work means that a couple move to a more luxurious and comfortable house. They have more money to spend, and their whole style of life changes. Occasionally this presents problems in that one spouse outgrows the other. The more successful husband or wife finds the partner of humble origins a burden and wishes to get rid of them. One comes across wives who have helped their husbands as students, or when putting their company together, who are treated as redundant when the husband succeeds later on.

Even more important to consider is downward social mobility, when a husband descends rather than ascends the ladder of success. This may be due to illness, drink, gambling, or sheer bad luck. It takes a lot of love to remain loyal to someone who appears a failure.

In fact, the problem of alcohol will feature in many families, and overcoming alcoholism may be a cross that has to be borne with fortitude and perseverance. Alcoholism in either spouse makes heavy inroads into the tranquillity of the home. Should a wife stay with an alcoholic husband? This is a question that only the individual wife can answer, but love does persevere and with patience alcoholic spouses have been cured.

53

Downward social mobility is especially present in protracted unemployment. Whether it is alcohol or unemployment, the consequence is a degree of poverty, and poverty is a challenge for loving. In poverty the commitment to the person rather than to things emerges, and, indeed, the commitment is the bond that survives all the social changes that supervene.

Emotional

Emotional patterns of change are hard to detect because they occur slowly over time, but one will be described in detail because it is present so often in marriage. This is the combination of a dependent spouse with a dominant partner. The dependent spouse starts the marriage needing guidance, encouragement and support. They lack confidence and they rely on their partner for encouragement and support. Either spouse can be dependent, but often it is the wife. She starts the marriage needing guidance over financial matters, her husband drives her around, he makes the important decisions, and she learns to trust his judgement.

This situation can go on for years, but gradually there is a shift. The wife has her children, and she looks after them effectively. She runs her house competently, and little by little confidence begins to emerge in her. She begins to take decisions on her own, to take initiatives, and even to go out to work, which strengthens her confidence even further. This growing confidence in the dependent personality is a feature which is seen in many marriages. Normally the husband welcomes it with open arms. This development means that the couple can share responsibility and face life together with renewed strength.

Occasionally the opposite occurs. The husband does not find the growth in his wife welcome. Her capacity to drive her car, manage her financial affairs, decide on holidays, handle her daily routine means that he has no power, no control over her. If he is insecure and feels that he can only hold on to her through her dependence, then her independence becomes a threat to his position. All this will be unconscious, but without realizing the reasons he will put obstacles in her way. If she expresses a wish to drive, he tells her that he has been driving her around all these years and why does she want to change now? If she enquires after financial matters he puts her down, he dismisses her with the remark that finances are not for women, and so every request is met with a refusal.

Under these circumstances such a wife has either to deny her growth and remain in a childlike dependence on her spouse, or leave him and choose someone else who will love her with her newly discovered confidence. The choice will be difficult, but this pattern of emotional growth dictates the fate of countless marriages.

Emotional changes from immaturity to maturity, dependence to independence, emotional coldness to emotional softness, dictate the future of many marriages. It is not that in the past these changes did not take place. The emotional developmental changes occurred, but the criterion by which marriages were judged was not the internal emotional encounter of the couple but the external social rectitude of roles. It is only now, with the shift from the external to the internal, that these changes play such a crucial role in the viability of marriages.

Under these circumstances love requires different criteria. The internal emotional world has to be understood and lived with. What has happened in the last thirty years is that, when initial patterns changed, partners changed each other as well. Divorce has risen out of all recognition because the emphasis has been placed on emotional fulfilment, and that requires a different understanding of marriage.

In addition to the changed emotional pattern of marriage, we have seen in this section that relationships may change and the marriage becomes based on new experiences. All this makes new demands on love, and the love–prayer dimension now requires patience, tolerance, education, understanding over emotional matters until some sort of convergence takes place in which the minimum needs of the couple are met.

Change over time may make people more cautious, guarded, less impetuous, more patient, understanding, caring and loving. Above all, people become 'more loving'. A great deal of divorce can be prevented if we are more patient and allow time for spouses to change and become more understanding and loving.

Intellectual

Change takes place intellectually as well. We shift gradually from intelligence to wisdom. We do this with the help of many people, but central to this change is the presence of our spouse who sees and hears our thoughts every day. The interaction between spouses allows for a deepening of thinking, checking out of details, intermixing of new ideas, and an ever more penetrating conclusion about the truth.

There may be alternative ways of increasing in intellectual stature. Spouses may find that, with the passage of time, they discover they have gifts unknown to them until now. In particular, wives may find that after the children are grown up or have left home, they discover new talents or interests.

Loving means that the spouse will facilitate the new gift in their partner. That may mean that the husband has to sacrifice his own position, his advance, in order for the wife to make good her own talents. These reversals of roles are part of the current loving scene in contemporary marriage.

Spirituality

It is perhaps appropriate to touch here upon the whole challenge of contemporary marriages. Loving is not so much a question of infatuation, physical and emotional attraction, as the capacity to care for an ever-changing person in one's spouse. The love–prayer dimension is found in a relationship in which feelings and emotions and sexual fulfilment are important, whilst they are forever changing within marriage. Love–prayer spirituality is the attempt to keep on caring for the continuously unfolding person.

There are two possibilities. Possibility number one is that the changes, however major, will still allow a retention of loving feelings and the support that that marriage needs is to help people understand these developments and attach to them loving feelings whilst they are happening. A degree of goodwill, hope and faith starts with every marriage. There are a few exceptions in which the marriage dissolves very quickly, but the majority of marriages start with a reservoir of goodwill. The whole challenge to the church and society is to help couples understand the social and emotional changes so that they can remain in touch with each other whilst the innovations take place. The nightmare is the situation where one spouse tries to persuade their partner to alter in a positive way which they refuse to do and ultimately give up trying; for example, the wife who tries to persuade her husband to give up drinking and he refuses. After a number of years she gives up trying and also gives up the marriage.

The second possibility is that when active love disappears in terms of feelings, emotions and sexual fulfilment, the relationship goes on in terms of caring. Caring is a form of love, and although less fulfilling than when active loving feelings are present, it is a way of keeping the relationship alive.

Conclusion

Change undoubtedly takes place during fifty years of marriage. Recently it has been suggested that to stay married to one person over such a long time is rather like a life sentence in prison. Mention has already been made that time is needed for healing, for deepening, sustaining and for growth into maturity. The love–prayer dimension is a way of ensuring that the couple stay together in the midst of struggle and pain to enjoy the ultimate result of permanence.

Reflection
- What major changes in your marriage have been positive experiences for you? What made them so?
- Which have at least threatened to undermine the relationship? How have you coped with these?
- How difficult do you think it is for married couples to cope successfully with major changes like the ones we have been discussing? What can help them?

Six

Sexual love

Of all the areas in marriage one would have thought that Christianity would be well advanced in linking sex with love. This has not been the case. In the early centuries of the church a dark cloud descended on sexuality, and people like Jerome and Augustine found it difficult to believe that there was anything good to be found in sexuality. So much so that for a very long time the only official acceptance of sex linked it with procreation.

In the course of this chapter we shall have to face the fact that the link between sex and procreation has been all but lost, and we will be seeking a new meaning to sex. In the meantime, it is worth noting that a major breakthrough took place on love and sex with the Second Vatican Council. These are the words of the Council:

> This love is uniquely expressed and perfected through the
> marital act. The actions within marriage by which the couple
> are united, intimately and chastely, are noble and worthy
> ones. Expressed in a manner that is truly human, these
> actions signify and promote that mutual self-giving by which
> spouses enrich each other with a joyful and a thankful will.

Nevertheless, the link between sex and children remains in the documents on marriage and family. 'Marriage and conjugal love are by their nature ordained towards the begetting and educating of children.'

Clearly this is not entirely the case. Sexual intercourse is needed on only a few occasions to create the required size of family. Also, coitus continues in the sixties, seventies and even eighties. The link between sexual intercourse and procreation has come to a historic halt. But no alternative has emerged. What is sex for? Is it for pleasure, or is it for love? This is the main challenge facing Western society.

The interpretation of sex for pleasure has meant an unprecedented sexual permissiveness. Young people have sexual intercourse soon after puberty, and hardly anyone enters cohabitation or marriage without having had sexual intercourse with somebody else. The wide availability of contraception has provided a passport to spontaneous sexual intercourse. Unfortunately a good deal of sex takes place without precaution, resulting in unwanted pregnancy and abortion. Part of the problem is that now that sex is no longer linked to procreation young people in particular find no reason why they should not indulge in it, and, I repeat, neither society nor the church has come up with an alternative sexual morality.

Sex and love

In this chapter an attempt will be made to link sex with love. Sexual attraction begins at puberty. At that time the boy is fascinated with the physical appearance of the girl, and the girl reciprocates with the boy. If we are not careful this erotic attraction remains the sole channel of communication between the sexes, so that every time a boy finds a girl attractive he wants to have sex with her.

But men and women are not just bodies; they are persons. By person I mean someone we have feelings for. We get attached to people because they have a value other than a sexual one. In having sex, we share the most personal aspect of ourselves; we would not dream of sharing our innermost secrets with someone unless we trusted them, felt deep feelings for them and wanted to share their life.

Sexual love is a matter of a meeting of bodies where hearts and minds have met before. When sex becomes a mere meeting of bodies, then there is only a partial meeting of persons. Basically sex has to have a meaning if it is going to be truly human. In the past its meaning was procreation, but that is gone, so its meaning must be to convey to another human being that they matter so much that we

59

want to share our life with them. Sex becomes the signature for personal commitment, commitment not to a body but to a person.

When we make love we become temporarily physically helpless as we engage in a deep exchange of pleasure leading to orgasm. If all we wanted was an orgasm then we could simply masturbate, but masturbation is a poor substitute for the personal sexual encounter. It is not a matter of having richer physical experience; it is a matter of being in the presence of another human being. The human being we have in our arms is our hope and destiny for our humanity, for our love. We want to give ourselves to someone who gives us meaning and purpose in our life.

Sexual intercourse as body language

When we are making love, we are speaking to each other with our bodies. We use the genitals as our language to say to each other precious things. What sort of things do we say to each other?

First of all, what we denote with our bodies is an acknowledgement that the person we make love to is someone we recognize as important, we appreciate as significant, and we show them with our bodies that we want them. In other words, we demonstrate that we recognize, appreciate and want them. In this sense sexual intercourse becomes the single most important affirmation of personhood. We cannot affirm personhood if we are in bed with different people on different nights. Then everybody is the same. Sex has ceased to have a special meaning.

Secondly, in the course of making love, we touch the erotic and non-erotic parts of the body of our partner, and in this way use them to convey pleasure to each other. In sexual intercourse the man makes the woman feel fully feminine, and her body becomes special for him. She becomes a special dedication of herself to him. In the same way the woman makes the man feel fully masculine by giving him sexual pleasure. She makes his body special, and it helps him to feel that he is offering the whole of his being to her. Thus sexual intercourse affirms each other's masculinity and femininity and joins them together into a new personal unity. It is an affirmation of sexual identity.

Thirdly, couples argue, quarrel and experience conflict with each other. Most of the time they forgive and forget pretty quickly. Occasionally the hurt is deeper and they have no ordinary means of forgiving. Temporarily the relationship has ruptured and the couple are alienated from each other. During this time they are so far apart that they cannot have sexual intercourse. Little by little the anger abates and they have sex. So sexual intercourse can become on certain occasions a means of reconciliation.

Fourthly, we are looking for personal meaning in life. We can be surrounded by material things, but material things need to have life breathed into them before they become alive. As far as our humanity is concerned, we need to come alive through another person. We need to feel that we matter. When our partner accepts our invitation to have sex with us, they do more than consent to join their bodies with ours. They do more than relieve sexual needs. In the course of intercourse they give us the deepest signal that we matter to them and they matter to us. It is a recurrent act which gives hope that another human being recognizes our existence. It is, when looked at in this way, a recurrent act of hope.

Fifthly, and finally, through sexual intercourse we give thanks to each other. We do this with our bodies. We say 'thank you' for being with us yesterday, today and hopefully tomorrow. It is a recurrent act of thanksgiving.

Morality and sexual intercourse

If these five communications are true, then sexual intercourse has an internal world of its own which is psychological and independent of procreation. It is a world of personal love. When a couple are making love they are talking to each other as persons with their bodies; this is the inner world of sexual meaning which demands that sex should take place in a setting of continuity, reliability and predictability. We are no longer concerned with a transient orgasm and the collection of sperm in a condom. We are concerned with the transmission of life in a deep and personal sense.

Sexual intercourse now becomes a personal act of love which can only be shared with someone who has shared your life. Its inner world of meaning gives it its new morality. You cannot share this richness with *any*body, but only with *some*body. This somebody, traditional Christianity maintained, was to be your husband or your wife. The basis for this exclusiveness was procreation, but we can see that there is a new basis for the exclusiveness which is personal love.

You cannot have these personal characteristics of love in

promiscuous relationships. You can only have them with some-body you know, you care for and you are committed to. So the new basis of sexual morality has to be partially procreation, in the sense that the children need the security and permanency of their parents, but even more important the morality has to depend on the intrinsic meaning of sex which is contained within the sexual act itself.

Prayer and sexual intercourse

In the traditional approach to sex, sexual intercourse was an indulgence to the instincts. It was often seen as forbidden fruit which was allowed to married couples. The emphasis, however, was on pleasure, and its satisfaction. The orgasm was the point the couple sought. Clearly pleasure plays a major part in sexual intercourse, but pleasure is the background to a personal encounter of love. When the couple are making love they are achieving the epitome of oneness in together-ness. They are making themselves fully available to each other. They are not only offering their bodies, but the whole of their being. It is a total consummation of selves.

All this is an active expression of prayer. It is reaching out to each other as the goal of mutual self-giving and faithfulness. Sexual inter-course is a mutual donation of everything we are. The prayer consists in reaching out to the other, appreciating the self of the other and making that person the goal of our love. It is total self-giving, and self-giving is at the centre of prayer. God so loved the world that he set it in motion. He so loved the world that he sent his only Son. Jesus so loved the world that he gave his life for it. Prayer is reaching out to the person we love.

Now sexual intercourse is *par excellence* a reaching out, and the consummation is oneness. In this oneness we receive the totality of the other into ourselves. St Paul understood something of this mystery when he wrote:

> For this reason, a man must leave his father and mother and
> be joined to his wife, and the two will become one body.
> This mystery has many implications; but I am saying it
> applies to Christ and the Church.
> (Ephesians 5:31–32)

The mystery which Paul alludes to is the unity of love between Christ and the church. This is a total fusion of love which Paul suggests takes place in the unity of sexual intercourse.

But there is one other aspect of theology that has to be considered. In sexual intercourse two people become one without losing their separate identity. This reflects the mystery of the Trinity in which three persons become one without losing their separate identity. Oneness in separateness and separateness in unity is what happens in sexual intercourse, and it gives us a clue of what occurs in the Trinity.

So sexual intercourse is far from being a forbidden fruit, an illicit pleasure that becomes licit in marriage. It is the central act of prayer in the daily liturgy of the domestic church. It is to the domestic church what the eucharist is to the community of the faithful in the building of the church at the local parish.

Physical care of sexual intercourse

Such a supreme act of love must not take place without due care and attention. It deserves respect and a great deal of effort. The world is full of literature which describes the sexual act. Often it borders on pornography. Pornography is, of course, the separation of the erotic from beauty and love. A few words of taking care to make sexual intercourse successful are not out of place when the description of the erotic is bathed in the love of the two people.

It should be remembered that sexual arousal has its roots in the male hormone testosterone. It circulates in both men and women and gives rise to sexual feelings that seek genital union. But love requires more than a discharge of sexual feelings, and this is particularly important for the man. There is more testosterone in the man, and usually a greater desire for sex.

The sexes differ in the setting in which they want to have sexual intercourse. The man may come home, have his meal, watch television and then see the thigh of his wife or the top of her breasts and want to have sex. The golden rule is to shift the emphasis from having sex to making love. For the wife, sex may be a physical excitation like that of her husband, but often the atmosphere has to be right. Sex for her is the culmination of the right atmosphere of the preceding twenty-four hours. She has to be in the right mood in which an atmosphere of love prevails in the home.

Having got the right setting, the couple can spend a little time preparing each other in the living room. I say in the living room because sex often takes place in the bedroom, but it does not have to.

It can take place anywhere. Given that the atmosphere is right, the couple can start to hug, caress and kiss each other. What they are saying to each other is that they are ready to make love. Psychologically this stage of preliminary preparation allows the secretion of fluids at the tip of the penis and in the vagina to lubricate the sites for sexual intercourse.

In moving to the bedroom there is more sexual excitation to be gained from seeing each other undress. In the winter a warm room adds to the atmosphere of physical relaxation. Seeing each other undress is not a question of peering at forbidden sites of the body. These sites have been put there by the Creator for the mutual relishing of the couple.

By now the couple may be fully sexually aroused. Usually this is the time when the whole point of the exercise is to arouse each other sexually. The husband may find it easier to be aroused than his wife. This is where stimulation of the erotic zones is important. The man usually enjoys having his penis rubbed by his wife, or the wife likes her breasts, particularly the nipples, to be touched, and especially her clitoris. The clitoris is the small, soft, rounded protrusion at the top of the vagina. This mutual stimulation of the erotic zones is not the stuff that Christians write about, but there is nothing to be embarrassed about, and we should proclaim this behaviour as part of the mutual joy of the couple given by God.

After the couple reach a degree of sufficient excitation they desire to become one. This is the moment of penetration, from which to-and-fro movements between the penis and vagina ultimately lead to the orgasm. The orgasm is the combination of a rising tide of sexual pleasure focused on the genitals. The orgasm is the pinnacle of excitation in which the man is flooded with sexual feelings and ejaculates sperm into the vagina. The woman gets a sense of intense spasms of pleasure, and the couple cling to one another in a mutual state of ecstasy. After the orgasm the couple rest in each other's arms and enjoy an after-climax flow of joy.

The whole sequence is not only an intense experience of pleasure, but it reinforces the loving that takes place at the level of sustaining, healing and growth. Sexual intercourse is the recurrent central prayer which integrates the rest of the life of prayer of the couple.

Sexual variations

If sexual intercourse has been a subject of silence amongst Christians, sexual variations have been an even greater taboo. They used traditionally to be called sexual deviations. Sexual deviations suggested the idea that these patterns of behaviour were distortions of normal sexual activity. In fact they are not distortions, but additional connections with sexual arousal.

Christians get confused when faced with sexual variations. They do not know what to do with these patterns of sexual behaviour. So there is a conspiracy of silence. Couples find out about their desires in their bedrooms and are confused as to how to react to their husbands or wives who present them with these wishes.

Usually the wishes are harmless. They are often part of the man's sexual arousal pattern, and prostitutes do a roaring trade from meeting the needs of men who are too embarrassed to make them known to their wives. The common heterosexual variations are the desires of men to see their wives dressed in black (or some other colour) underclothes, or in soft furry materials, or in rubber. The whole range of these smooth materials is sexually exciting.

Next and more complicated is the desire of the man to dress himself in women's underclothes. Some men have to parade in the privacy of their bedroom with such underclothes, and have sexual intercourse in them.

Even more complicated, and less well understood, is the desire which can apply to both sexes, to associate sexual arousal with the infliction of pain (sadism) or the reception of pain (masochism). These are complex variations in which men and women want to be tied, beaten or humiliated in some way.

All this material of sexual arousal has gone underground; it is not discussed in ordinary Christian circles, and it has often been left to prostitutes to cater for such needs. This is a pity. Most of these desires, which are called fetishes, can become part and parcel of ordinary lovemaking without any loss of dignity or sexual integrity if both partners are able to accept them; there may be problems when what arouses one partner upsets the other, and help may be needed. But provided pain and suffering are avoided, and everything that is done has the full consent of each partner, sexual pleasure is part and parcel of God's plan for human love.

Infidelity

Infidelity, or adultery, is the situation when a spouse in a marriage has a sexual affair with a third party. Affairs have increased and they are part and parcel of the permissive sexual scene of our day. The main point about adultery used to be that there was a risk of pregnancy outside the marriage, with the uncertainty of who the father was and the risk of resources which belonged to the marriage being transferred outside the home.

The advent of effective contraceptives has made pregnancy less likely. So the essential element of adultery is less the risk of pregnancy and more the betrayal of the trust of the marital relationship.

A spouse whose partner has an affair feels let down in that it is not the material resources that are transferred but the love that belongs to the spouse, that is given to somebody else. This is expressed as a sense of loss by the partner and building up trust again takes a long time.

It is customary to allocate blame and responsibility to the person who has the affair. In this way when the spouse forgives the issue is settled with the guilt of the person who commits the adultery, and the magnanimity of the injured party. But this is not always a reflection of the truth. Sometimes we have to ask what was missing in the relationship that led to the affair. When infidelities are examined, it is not unusual to find that the so-called 'innocent' party is partially responsible for what happened. So forgiveness has often to be mutual.

Conclusion

Sexual intercourse is the deepest expression of personal love, and in the setting of the domestic church is the central prayer in the liturgical life of the couple. It involves the deepest emotional layers of the couple, and the tendency to hide from others the secrets of the sexual life is an outward manifestation of the inner world of deep love that is generated.

Sexuality is a subject that has had a bad press in Christianity, but in fact it brings into being the deepest moments of the unity between the physical and the personal, and it incarnates for the couple what the incarnation captured in God's love for humankind.

Prayer-notes

Experience Reflect on the extent to which sex has become for you 'the signature of personal commitment: commitment not to a body but a person'.

Pointers-to-depth The whole of Scripture is a story of God's personal commitment ('covenant') to us, enacted through *physical* things. It is also a story of *intimate mutuality*.

To recall how physical, we can think, for example, of:

- Jesus' life, his stories, his meals, his death;
- the Song of Songs celebration/evocation of sexual intimacy in the Bible;
- 'the Word became *flesh*'.

Response Can you, as married partners, make your sexual intercourse a deeper expression of your love: your commitment to sustain and heal and forgive each other, to grow together, to rejoice in the gift of your intimate sharing?

Seven

The growth of love

In the past the ends of marriage were defined in terms of the primary end, as the procreation and education of children; the secondary end was defined as mutual help and the relief of concupiscence. The secondary end has now been translated into love as experienced through sustaining, healing and growth, and through sexual intercourse. This has been a reconsideration of personal relationships through the eyes of dynamic psychology. It is now time to have an outline of the primary end seen through dynamic psychology. In this chapter I want to take the reader through the main stages of the growth of love in the child. It should be noted that it is merely an outline because a detailed account would be a book in itself. The love that is generated in the intimacy of childhood is relived in the intimacy of the couple in marriage.

The first year of life

When a baby is born it finds itself in a world in which it does not feel it belongs. It is a mass of needs which on the surface appear to be all physical, and yet its most important requirements are emotional. It needs to belong and to have a relationship of love in order to survive. In the last half-century it has been shown that if babies are physically nurtured but do not have a relationship of love they sicken and die. So how do they form this relationship of love?

It has been established that what a baby does when it is born is to form an affective attachment with its mother. This means that it creates an emotional link with mother and then father. Emotions become the basis of love. This attachment is formed through three physical dimensions.

The first is touch. The baby holds on to mother, and the mother holds the baby. This is a tactile encounter of safety which is mediated through touch. The second is vision. The baby quickly identifies the face of the mother, and then gradually the rest of her body. The mother is for the baby a signal of security and gradually one of pleasure and joy. The third is sound. The baby recognizes the voice of the mother and can call her at any time through crying. Crying is a powerful signal which brings most mothers to the side of their baby.

In this way, through touch, sound and vision we form an attachment with another which is the beginning of love. We should need no reminder that we fall in love with people through vision, sound and touch. We are attracted by the appearance of another person, the sound of their voice and the feel of their body. I have mentioned repeatedly in the previous chapter that the body is no mere collection of physical entities, but a unity of the physical, the emotional and the spiritual.

From the very beginning the baby experiences a combination of the physical, the emotional and the spiritual and, as its relationships with other people unfold throughout life, there is an integrated response whenever another person is met. The other person is holy by the very hold they have on life. Life is holy and when we meet another person a spiritual encounter takes place. Baptism confirms what is inherent in everybody, the life of the spirit.

In the same first year of life the baby not only forms an attachment to the mother and father, it not only forms the foundation of all future attachments of love, but it also deepens its sense of trust. The sense of trust develops first through the physical security that the baby experiences in the arms of its mother and father. This physical security is enhanced by the fact that there is a routine of feeding, washing, sleeping, which the baby gets accustomed to. The trust is extended as it can bring mother to its side by crying. The world takes on the shape of being reliable and predictable, building a network of safety. This network of safety will extend when verbalization begins to take place in the next two years. To physical

69

relationship will now be added verbal veracity and the beginnings of truth will dawn in the life of the child.

Second and third year of life

The second and third years of life are loaded with psychological developments which are pertinent to love. This is the beginning of the gradual separation between mother and child. The toddler will amass a whole range of new abilities. It will quickly learn to stand up, to crawl and to walk. The ability to walk will in fact take it away from the mother into the next room, where it will play quietly for some time. Playing alone may not be a very exciting event from the point of view of the adult but the child needs to master some major psychological abilities.

It needs to be able to carry the image of mother within itself in her physical absence. In other words it needs to internalize her so that it can feel safe and be left by itself – this process of internalization is a major step in human development. If the toddler did not internalize mother, it would not be able to leave her side, and the process of gradual separation could not take place.

In fact, there are children who cling to mother well beyond the stage when they should be playing on their own. School phobia is a neurosis in which children cannot leave home and go to school. Finally, mention has already been made of adults who are afraid to be left on their own, and cling to their spouses. The origins for all these problems begin at this stage of development.

Adults also have to internalize their loved ones. Every time we leave home in the morning we carry within us the picture of our spouse. We carry more than a picture; we have a sense of them because we internalize them. One reason why affairs occur when people go abroad is that some men and women do not have a clear definition of their beloved inside them. A telephone call or a letter may help, but some people pine for the comfort of a real human being who can be seen, heard and touched. The need for a substitute person can be very real. On the surface the apparent explanation is the resort to sex but, as we have seen, sex is a means of reaching another person and that person can give security. So we carry our loved ones inside us throughout the day, and we return home to renew their reality in the flesh.

Internalization is closely linked with the process of grieving.

When the child leaves the room where mother is it goes off feeling secure but if it hurts itself, or a stranger appears, it soon runs back to mother. Almost invariably mother is there to soothe it. But if, for some reason, she is no longer there, the toddler will cry. This is the protest of the child at the absence of the mother. The protest can go on for long periods and then, if the mother does not reappear, the crying will cease.

There will come a point when crying will be no longer fruitful. At this point there will be no more protest or anger. There will simply be detachment. The youngster will lose contact with mother. When long stays in hospital were the order of the day and mothers were not encouraged to visit their children frequently, then emotional detachment took place. Children lost meaningful contact with their mother. They looked happy on the surface but there was deep distress underneath, and when contact was re-established with mother, attachment had to be formed afresh.

Grieving is basically connected with loss and separation. When someone close to us dies we begin the process of grieving by crying. This is our protest. It is followed by anger that the person who left us could do such a thing. Thirdly, we detach ourselves emotionally from the beloved, but, unlike the child, the adult does not leave it at that. The process of internalization means that we can live the reality of the deceased within us. We can actually sense their presence inside us and, although they are physically absent, they are emotionally present.

There is one more aspect of internalization which concerns faith itself. God is a reality we cannot see, hear or touch, so how do we get our faith? How do we believe in him? This happens through the process of internalization. From the second year onwards children are given stories about Jesus, particularly at Christmas. These stories activate a picture of a living Being who is gradually internalized – we have a sense of God without seeing, touching or hearing his existence. Those who do not believe in God make his silence and deafness the proof of his non-existence. But those who believe have a secure sense of God's existence inside them.

The final psychological experience of these years is the presence of conflict. The toddler wants to do things its own way, and the mother and father have their own ideas of how things should be done. Most of the time they win but at regular intervals the toddler rebels. Then there follows a shout, or even a smack. For a moment, and for the toddler a few seconds can be a very long time, the assumed heaven of mother is taken away. There is a bleak chill. Within a very short time there is forgiveness and reconciliation. The sequence of conflict, anger, rupture of the relationship, guilt, forgiveness and reconciliation is one with which all humanity is familiar. It begins at this stage of life and remains essentially the same throughout life.

Fourth and fifth years of life

As the child proceeds to the fourth and fifth years, it acquires a momentum of its own. The child roams around the garden, climbs trees and intrudes into the life of its parents. It is time for initiations, and the home reverberates with the question, Why? Why this? Why that? The child is capable of limited understanding, but it is part of the love exchange that, while the knowledge imparted should not exceed the capacity of the child to understand, nevertheless the parents should always respect the truth. Sharing the truth is part of the trust the child places in the parents and, through them, places in the whole world.

Part of the child's experience at this time is the acquisition of the meaning of good and bad. These words surround the child from the time it is born. The word 'good' surrounds all moments of approval, and 'bad' all moments of disapproval. Gradually the words begin to penetrate the child's consciousness that 'good' is associated with goodness and 'bad' with badness. Goodness and badness in turn are linked with the child's self-esteem, with feeling lovable. Self-esteem and lovability are linked.

Mention has been made already of two experiences of love of self or self-esteem. The first is the reception of the experience of unconditional love. The child feels loved because it exists, not because of what it has done or achieved. It is true that feelings of goodness are shown when food is eaten properly, when toilet training is being achieved, when obedience is realized, and so on. The praise that is received at these moments is a passive experience of feeling loved because one exists. It is not felt that goodness is the pursuit of one's exploration and one's own achievement. This state of unconditional love of self, felt in the first stage of intimacy, is crucial for feeling loved and loving in subsequent relationships of love. In the experience of love in adult life we can feel loved because we have done something worthwhile or we can bask in the love that has not been earned but has been bestowed upon us because we simply exist.

In these critical years the child learns the beginning of this unconditional love which endures for the rest of life. How deep and penetrating unconditional love is felt depends on how deep, consistent and *enduring* is the love offered to the child. It is an important love to feel because it is the basis of feeling loved subsequently; it is also the basis for feeling loved by God. We cannot earn God's love, nothing that we achieve can give us any justification for feeling loved, but we can feel fully loved because we are cherished by God who wants nothing but our good.

The school years – the primary school

Sometime between the fourth and fifth year children begin to go to school. School is a world of order, work, settling in a new community and of rules and regulations. The child learns how to cope within the wider setting of a larger community. Within this community there is competition and achievement. The three Rs are mastered, but what enters deeply into the child's consciousness is the goodness, the glow, the good feelings achieved through results. Every child becomes slowly conscious of a hierarchy of achievement in which its own achievements are measured against those of the others.

There are important implications for one's love life as a result of the acquisition of self-esteem from these two different sources. The first source is the unconditional and unearned love which is learned from our parents; the second is what is acquired through our own efforts. Normally self-esteem is dependent on both these sources. So that when the self-esteem gained from one's productivity fails for any reason, such as unemployment, sickness, old age, failure, then one can remain buoyant on the self-esteem of unconditional love from those who surround us, and from God.

That is the normal way of things, but sometimes things go wrong. There are men and women who grow up with little or no sense of unconditional love. They rely entirely on the love they earn for themselves. When this is going well, they feel good. Such men and women depend primarily on work for their self-esteem. When work fails for one reason or another they are doubly bereft and are plunged into despair. In fact, psychologists have to deal with the small percentage of men and women who have never been loved and who are not good at work, so that both systems of raising self-esteem fail. In these circumstances depression and despair face the person and out of the ranks of such individuals suicidal attempts and suicide occur.

In these years of primary school another development takes place which is significant for our personality. Round about seven or eight children challenge the authority of their parents. Authority is in fact challenged much earlier on but children on the whole comply with what parents want. At about seven or eight children want an explanation and justification of what parents request. They want to be satisfied that the request is not an arbitrary demand but something related to reality.

This is the time when home and school reverberate with the phrase 'It's not fair'. Fairness is something the child yearns for, and from about the end of the first decade onwards we are all primed towards a society and personal relationships of fairness. This is where law and justice begin to operate. Children begin to appreciate that life is not black and white; there are in fact extenuating circumstances. In the midst of extenuating circumstances there is a hunger for justice. Love and justice are intimately linked and the home needs to have equitable relationships between all its members so that love is seen to pervade throughout the whole household.

Puberty

At about eleven children leave the primary school to enter the secondary school. It is the first step of adult education. Adulthood is approaching and with this, puberty. Puberty arrives with the secondary sexual characteristics. The boy's testicles descend to the scrotum and enlarge. The penis enlarges. The face is covered with hair and the voice breaks. The girl's breasts enlarge, as does her vagina, and she begins menstruation.

From now on the boy and the girl separate sexually from their parents, and look towards each other for sexual attraction and social fulfilment. This is the incest taboo. It means that sexual relationship between children and their parents is prohibited. This prohibition is on the whole well preserved, but there are occasional breaches, and sexual abuse is a major concern of our age.

In the previous chapter emphasis was placed on the fact that sex was for love, and it is worth returning to this point again. We have seen in this chapter how from the time we are born we received a personal encounter of love. Our whole life until puberty is orientated towards personal love. By this I mean that the signals we receive from each other are tokens of interpersonal recognition and appreciation. We are not orientated towards bodies, but to persons. We are not orientated to any persons, but to persons we love and who love us.

At puberty we still remain attached to our parents, brothers and sisters, but sexually we have to find someone outside the family to become sexually bonded. This is what sexual integrity is about. It is possible to relate at puberty to other bodies simply as bodies and have sex indiscriminately. The whole point of the description in this chapter is that we grow up to orientate to persons, and to persons who love us. Thus sex ultimately belongs to a union of the physical and the personal.

The second half of the second decade deals with the final separation between adolescents and parents. This separation consists of finishing school, leaving home and starting work or continuing with education as an adult.

The stage has now been reached for courtship and marriage and the whole cycle of love begins again.

Reflection
● What do these stages of growth suggest to you about:
   – the nature or 'ingredients' of love?
   – the importance of loving relationships, for everyone?
   – your responsibilities in this matter:
      for the members of your family?
      for those who feel unloved?
   – how far St Paul's 'The whole Law is summed up in one
      commandment: "Love your neighbour as you love
      yourself" ' takes us to the centre of the human story?
      (Romans 13:9; Galatians 5:14)

Prayer-notes
Experience Reflect on your own experience of loving and of being loved: both the successes and the failures.

Pointers-to-depth Read a few times this Old Testament portrait of God – the centre of all human life:

> With tender kindness I have compassion for you.
> The mountains may depart,
> the hills be shaken,
> but my tender kindness for you will never be shaken,
> and my covenant of peace will never be shaken,
> says God, the compassionate.
> (Isaiah 54:8, 10)

Response Could you, through a few minutes of quiet reflection on such passages each day, live more from the *centre* of your life?

Eight

Divorce

The whole emphasis in this Part of this book is concerned with the domestic church as the family in an extended love–prayer dimension. However, we know that love is not the only prevailing state of marriage. Marriages can exist in conditions of indifference, in fluctuating moods of closeness and alienation, in interludes of wellbeing and of anger; finally they may end in divorce or separation.

There has always been marital breakdown. What is new about the current situation is its scale. In 1857 civil divorce started in England and Wales and up to the beginning of the Second World War the number involved was a few thousand. After the Second World War the numbers climbed to nearly 50,000, and then by 1960 they dropped to about 25,000. In 1969 the new Divorce Act came in and the numbers soared. But even before the Divorce Act, which made irretrievable breakdown of the marriage the sole criterion for divorce, numbers had begun to rise.

Currently numbers for Britain fluctuate around the 160,000 mark; that is, nearly 40 per cent of marriages end in divorce. In parts of the USA nearly 75 per cent of marriages end in divorce, and in Russia 60 per cent. In Britain, when the children under sixteen are taken into account, some 500,000 men, women and children are involved in divorce each year.

This is a tragedy on a large scale. Before we can do something about it, we have to try to understand it. There are three ways of understanding divorce on such a scale. First, there are global factors. Secondly, there are sociological factors, and thirdly, there are patterns of problems which arise which lead specifically to marital breakdown. I shall deal with each one in turn.

Global forces

The first factor to be considered amongst the global forces is the emancipation of women. Women have come of age and are not prepared to subject themselves to behaviour which is unacceptable but which would have been acceptable two or three generations ago. Secondly, and very important, marriage, as described already, is shifting from being a contract of social obligation to becoming an emotional encounter between men and women. This change from clearly delineated social roles to a world of emotional satisfaction is a particularly challenging transition. The fact is that we have not learned the skills to negotiate these emotional demands and the relationship takes a downhill trend when couples are glad to see the back of each other. Thirdly, both men and women have higher expectations of their marriage than ever before. Fourthly, the preventive mechanisms such as religion and moral commitment have been reduced in intensity.

Thus a host of factors have come together to enlarge the scale of marital breakdown. These forces have not slackened and it is imperative that they are understood if effective action is to be taken to reduce the rate of marital breakdown.

Social and psychological factors

Within these global factors, sociologists have discovered a number of social factors which make individuals particularly vulnerable to divorce. The first factor is age. Individuals who get married under the age of twenty are particularly liable to marital breakdown. Sociologists have discovered that, whereas the final person we choose is a mystery, we tend to define the field of eligibles from the same social, economic and educational background as ourselves. When we cross these boundaries and mixed marriages ensue, the risks of divorce are enhanced. Finally, there is an increased relationship between social class and marital breakdown. The lower the socio-economic group, the higher is the risk of divorce.

As far as psychological factors are concerned, the evidence points to higher rates of marital breakdown when one or both spouses have personality disorders, such as immaturity or psychopathy.

Individual factors

In several publications the author has delineated a system whereby marital breakdown has been linked with five elements, namely, the sociological, emotional, sexual, intellectual and spiritual. These five factors will be described in three stages of marriage. The first stage comprises the first five years. The second stage comprises the next twenty years from 30 to 50, and the third stage from 50 until the death of one spouse.

First stage

1. *Sociological*
There are five sociological factors that are associated with marital breakdown.

The first is the spouses' *relationship with their parents*. Marriage is an intimate relationship in which the couple interact primarily with one another. The parents are there to give advice if asked and to help if needed, but the dependence on the parents for survival is over. There are spouses, however, who have never broken their emotional ties with their parents. They marry, but the point of reference in their life is their parents, whom they telephone or contact constantly. Every little problem is referred to them and their advice is sought on matters that should be discussed between the partners. In this way the husband or wife is bypassed, and there is really no marriage.

The second factor is *the running of the household*. When couples are courting, sometimes the moon is promised. After the marriage it is usually the husband who fails to keep his bargain, and it is not unusual for the wife to be left to run the house, work, and look after the children. Working and running the home may in themselves be too much, let alone when the children arrive. The consequence of having to do all this is tiredness and irritability, leading to frequent quarrels, and in no time there is disenchantment with the marriage.

The third factor is *money*. Couples can marry and find that one of them is poor at handling money. This is not an uncommon happening, and with time and patience can be adjusted. However, money has wider connotations. Money means three things. It has an absolute economic value; in other words, there must be enough to go around. It has an emotional value: 'If you loved me you would not keep me short'. Thirdly, it has power. The person who holds the purse has power over their partner. Money can cause trouble in any of these three ways.

The fourth factor is *work*. Work can destabilize a marriage in one or two ways. The spouse can work too hard and is then often late or rarely available for socializing. The other position is unemployment. Unemployment has been shown to be damaging to marriage. The self-esteem of the individual drops and they become depressed, irritable and angry. They may drink too much, and a vicious circle is established which leads to the deterioration of the relationship.

The fifth factor is *leisure*. This is something that applies again to the husband. He will marry and have all the advantages of marriage, but when it comes to spare time he will go to the pub or play his favourite sport, leaving the wife and children at home. This causes a great deal of distress at the beginning of marriage.

2. *Emotional*

There are a few marriages that end weeks or months after the wedding. A startled spouse is faced with a partner who does not know why but wants to leave. If pressed to give a reason they cannot. Nothing is wrong with their partner. They just cannot cope with being married. A deeper examination of the person will often show that marriage is experienced as the object of a phobia, a state which is stifling them. They cannot cope with the closeness of the relationship, and they depart to the dismay of their young spouse.

Another emotional issue is the projecting on to the spouse of the characteristics of a parental figure. The wife is pushed to be like his mother, or the husband is pushed to be like her father. Naturally, in these situations the wife and the husband object to being pigeon-holed. They want to be independent people who run their own life in their own way.

Yet another emotional pattern is ambivalence. In other words, the spouse marries their partner on the basis of, say, dominance;

at the conscious level they want to be dominated, but at the unconscious level they rebel and fight their partner for the very qualities they so admire. Ambivalence is a widespread phenomenon.

Emotionally spouses may be discovered early on to be cold and unexpressive, and this takes the partner by surprise.

Immaturity may be another factor that appears early in the marriage. By immaturity is meant a combination of factors, such as overdependence on parents, difficulty in making decisions, impulsiveness, being quick to anger, oversensitive to criticism, unreliable on time-keeping, incapable of handling authority, and a hankering after imaginary and unrealistic goals. The immature person is really unable to take on the responsibility of the adult relationship in marriage.

3. Sexual

The most obvious sexual difficulty in the first stage of marriage is non-consummation. This is a problem in which the wife finds vaginal penetration too painful and cannot accept it. Or the husband may suffer from impotence or premature ejaculation. These are difficulties that can be easily overcome, and couples with such difficulties should seek expert advice.

Sexual intercourse itself can be disappointing to some wives or husbands, but particularly to wives. It may take some time for the couple to get accustomed to each other's needs. The usual problem is that the husband wants frequent sex without paying enough attention to the emotional side of sexual intercourse, and the wife finds her husband's incessant demands unattractive. Adaptation takes place when the husband realizes that his wife needs an emotional background to sex, and the wife appreciates the physicality of her husband.

After the birth of a baby the wife may go off sex temporarily. The desire for sex soon returns, but sometimes the lack of sexual desire is part and parcel of a post-childbirth depressive syndrome. In these instances women become depressed, irritable, lose their libido, may lose or put on weight, and suffer from poor sleep. Post-childbirth syndromes sap the life from a marriage and expert help should be sought to overcome this problem.

Affairs may occur in these early years, and they may involve men and women who were close friends before the marriage. They can be very disruptive and should be taken seriously, with help sought.

4. Intellectual and spiritual

A lack of intellectual and spiritual compatibility may not be discovered until a couple have been together for some time; novelty and a superficial getting to know each other may have hidden this before. This is less likely if the couple have known each other, or even lived together, for a longer period before marriage.

Second stage: from 30 to 50

1. Sociological

The single most important factor of these years is change. The sociological change is the movement upwards of the couple if they have prospered, in which case one spouse may leave their partner behind and no longer find them a suitable person in the dizzy heights they have achieved. The opposite result is downward mobility into poverty through business failure, drink, gambling, or inadequacy. In these circumstances marriages break up because there is no energy left to sustain them.

2. Emotional

As I have mentioned already, the most likely problem emotionally is that one or the other spouse outgrows their partner. Thus the dependent spouse becomes independent, the immature spouse becomes mature, the cold spouse becomes warm, and each one of them outgrows their partner. Alternatively the spouse finds the dependence, immaturity, or schizoid personality intolerable.

3. Sexual

The sexual problems of these two decades consist of these common male ones of impotence and premature ejaculation, with loss of sexual desire for both sexes and anorgasmia, with dyspareunia, or painful intercourse, for wives. It is, of course, during these two decades that affairs escalate and the aftermath of an affair ranges from resolution of conflict and forgiveness to actual separation.

4. Intellectual and spiritual

In this phase the couple may develop different ideologies, opinions, outlooks, and go their separate ways. Usually they converge and build a new basis for relationships.

Third stage

In the third stage the departure of the children allows the couple to reassess their position. They may have become increasingly distant from each other and now that the children have gone may find it a convenient time to separate.

Sexually the single most important issue of this phase for women is the menopause. The menopause does not alter sexual desire, and sexual intercourse may continue uninterrupted for the next thirty or so years. What may affect the couple is the husband's impotence. Marriages continue to break down during these decades, but with less frequency. Intellectually and spiritually the alienation of the preceding phase may continue.

The consequences of divorce

Divorce has been proceeding on such a scale for the last thirty years that there has been time to study it. There are some husbands and wives who are delighted to have left the matrimonial home. The pain and misery of the arguments, the anger, the sheer impossibility of the situation, make the break a welcome relief. So when divorce is discussed there are always men and women who are positive about their freedom.

But when it is looked at *en masse* the results are terribly depressing. Study after study has shown that the divorced fare poorly both psychologically and in their physical health. The evidence points to adverse health consequences in terms of cancer, heart disease, accidents, suicidal attempts and suicide itself. In all these areas divorced people do worse than those who have remained married. Second marriages also have a higher risk of breakdown than first ones. All in all, it is much better to try to stay together with your first spouse if you can.

The children also suffer. There is good accumulated evidence that children from divorced homes do worse socially, economically and educationally, and in turn their own marriages have a higher rate of divorce. Stepchildren fare badly also. These are all statistical results; nothing can be said about an individual child, but all the indications point in the direction of a heavy price for divorce.

The divorced person

There are millions of divorced people. What can we offer them in a book about the domestic church, love and prayer? What is the constructive approach?

The divorced person may have stayed in good relationship with their ex-spouse, and between them they may be attending to their children in a friendly, constructive way. The harmonious post-divorce relationship of parents is the best guarantee for the upbringing of the children. However, there are ex-spouses who cannot stand the sight of each other, and enmity continues long after the divorce.

The period after the divorce may be different for the husband and the wife. The wife is often better able to look after herself and the children in practical ways, though she may be worse off financially. Men on the whole fare worse after divorce, but there are, of course, lots of exceptions.

This period after divorce is one of grieving. There may be protest by the spouse who does not want the divorce. Protest may be accompanied by a great deal of crying, sorrow and depression. This depression lifts after some months or, in some cases, after a year or two. There may also be anger, persistent anger at the partner, or anger with oneself for having let things reach such a pitch. This anger may continue over a long time, or it may dissolve. Finally, there is the phase of detachment in which the spouse is incorporated into one's being, and there are pleasant and positive memories, or a gradual fading of the part they played in one's life. The married years can never be completely eliminated, but the emotional colour they take will vary from person to person.

In the meantime life must continue. If there are children, they have to be attended to, and so has work. Living as a divorced person has its difficulties. Being invited to parties, socializing, may not be easy. Here the support of the family, if one has one, is immensely important, as are the friends one keeps.

What about the divorced person's faith? Throughout my section I have seen religion in terms of love. The love–faith dimension has to go on. The most important thing to realize in the midst of adversity is that you remain lovable. Divorce is not a crime. We remain people with self-esteem. That must not diminish. This self-esteem comes from our work, from our friends, from our family and, above all, from God. If we are divorced we are no less important in God's eyes.

Then we have to think about the future. That depends on what age we are when we get divorced, the circumstances of our divorce, and whether we want to remain single, cohabit or remarry. All these steps will have their challenges. Before we decide what to do with our lives, we have to learn from the past. We have to learn from our previous marriage. What kind of person are we, and what kind of life do we want to lead? An examination of our personality and the factors which led to the breakdown of our marital relationship is an essential consideration prior to taking the next step in our life.

Nine

The Christian community

What can our Christian community do to bring about the vision presented in this Part on marriage? There can be little doubt that, if the church was seen to highlight ordinary experiences in terms of love and to convert them into prayer, then it would respond far more accurately to the everyday needs of human beings.

Men and women have a natural link between the physical, emotional and spiritual. From the moment we are born our interpersonal links of love reflect the interpersonal reality of love of the Trinity. When human beings are in relationship with each other they are living the life of love of the Trinity and, provided we rightly interpret how that love is lived in human terms, then we have a living connection between this life and God. When men, women and children are loving each other, they are living the inner life of God and so the everyday experience of family life is a liturgy of prayer.

This is a vision which I would like to see widely shared. If God is love, as John would have us believe, then all our human transactions of loving place us in the heart of the mystery of God. God has been seen as a judge, as a source of authority, as a source of punishment, and these traits have provided a deep sense of guilt, so that Christianity is often seen as a faith of judgement, guilt and reparation. Very often Christians feel that their only contact with God is achieved when they feel bad. The aim should be to help people recognize that they are in contact with God when they are *loving*.

How is this to be done with marriage and the family? Clearly we need a vision of the link between love and God. In theory it exists; in practice people are more conscious of God at times of failure, than when they are turning to others in love. So the beginning of understanding may be at school. There the link between love and God has to be forged. It has to be forged in the understanding of human development and the efforts we make to love and be loved.

So a local church should try to encourage the programmes of human relationships that are present in the local schools and in the local youth organizations where young people in their teens can come to understand the exciting link between love and God.

After the stage of school and youth clubs there is the phase of premarital preparation. This is undoubtedly the time for a spiritual understanding of the sacrament as a covenant, but the special link between human love and God needs emphasizing.

Young people have to be helped to understand the progress of love from falling in love to loving, and the need for sustaining, healing and growth. They need to link their sexual love with God as a life-giving force to the growth of their personalities. The premarital course should be the beginning of a programme of education in the life of love of the couple and their children.

There follows the wedding itself. Historically the wedding was seen as the beginning and the end of marriage. In the course of the wedding the couple give the rights of their body formally to each other and make a mutual life commitment. This is a commitment to love each other. Seen in this way, the wedding is not an end but a beginning. The church should see the wedding as a beginning of a life-long journey in which the couple are supported in their growth of love for each other.

Following the wedding come the early years of marriage. Research has shown that these years are crucial for the stability of marriage. It is a time when the marital relationship is consolidating and the couple are evaluating the quality of their love for each other. It is a significant period when they need special help to make the relationships work. How can the local community help with this process?

The early years could be an opportunity to bring the couple together and assess their needs as the relationship is unfolding. In those areas where it is possible, groups of couples should form to discuss their developing viewpoints. When children arrive, attempts can be made to organize babysitting rotas, playgroups, crèches, so that the young mothers have an opportunity to meet and discuss their experiences. This is the time when programmes for communication should be made available so that the skills of relationship are enhanced. The development of skills for contemporary relationships is a matter of priority in these early years.

As the children progress to school, the school can share the responsibility for providing opportunities for the enhancement of the parents' skills in relating to each other.

Returning to the local church, there is a need for liturgical events to celebrate marriage. This is an opportunity for composing liturgies in which the Scriptures and the experience of the couple are brought together. The life of commitment can be linked to the covenant, the erotic to the Song of Songs, love to the gospel and epistles of St John, adultery to the passage in John on the woman taken in adultery, and so on. There is no lack of spiritual material which can be linked to contemporary marriage.

Another possible event is the celebration every month of an anniversary Eucharist for all the marriages with anniversaries in that month.

The parish could also devise its own events to bring the love of married life to the fore. In doing this, it should of course be careful not to appear to be devaluing the life experience of its unmarried members, for the whole point is an attempt to make the people of God conscious that their daily life of love is their domestic church, *the* place where they find God in their life.

PART THREE
EMPLOYED IN ORGANIZATIONS
Ten

How our work can be good news

'It's like the Army, only worse', is how Bill sums up his work. In the supermarket where he works he is simply told to follow a drill. 'Don't talk. Don't think. Don't take initiatives. And, above all, don't ask why things are run this way: headquarters know best.'

Some of Bill's workmates think that's unfair to the modern army. Like any firm, the army requires discipline, but it treats the soldiers as persons. However, they agree with Bill's assessment of their workplace: 'You're just a cog in the machine'.

What makes this worse for these people is that some of their friends work in supermarkets or smaller stores locally which go out of their way to avoid a drill-like regime. Jane, for example, works in Halfords. The other day she was proud to hear a motor-bike enthusiast describing what it's like to shop there. 'When I go in there, an assistant will either discover for me what I want or they will suggest that I want something different because I haven't understood the problem. Or, if they haven't got it, they will tell me what to do next about the problem. So, need I tell you why I go into Halfords in preference to other places?'

Jane knows that that standard of service hasn't come about by chance. In all the 450 branches of Halfords round the country the staff take the first hour of a working day off once a week to look together at how they're operating and why. They build up their sense of being a team of responsible and capable people who really want to help the customers. The firm's aims are explained and their own suggestions are welcomed.

The kind of experience Jane is having could become the norm. Many employers are now aware that old army-type methods damage a firm. Employees may agree to follow a drill if they need the job, but they won't feel commitment to the firm that imposes it and put their backs into the work. The quality of the product or service will suffer. The employer may have a well-disciplined set of zombies at his command, but he'll soon lose his customers to firms where the employees feel motivated to tackle their work more positively.

What employers are having to cope with is that, in the last few decades, many things have changed. The new technology increasingly forces them to employ a more sophisticated workforce. These people are accustomed to taking responsibility and having views on how organizations they are involved in should be run.

Also, in an increasing number of firms, relatively junior employees *have* to take responsibility, whether the boss wants that or not. An employee may have access to all the relevant information – because it's on the computer. In addition, now that firms contract out much more, a quite junior employee may be dealing with a whole range of suppliers and collaborators. That employee builds up a knowledge of them, through experience, that nobody else has. If the management refuses to put most of the responsibility in that employee's hands, faulty decisions are bound to occur.

Factors like this are beginning to force employers to treat their workforce as people who can use their gifts responsibly – and many employers care enough about their workforce to want to do that anyway. But the strongest motivation can come from the everyday experience of work in firms where that happens.

Of course there remain in such firms the monotony, the hard work, the misunderstandings, envy and resentments. But, to a substantial degree, these are felt differently because of a more human, 'family' context. My fellow-workers and my boss have become less machines that work the system than people with different gifts, approaches, even quirks, who contribute their own 'thing' with some pride and joy to what we're all doing. It is *people* I'm now in touch with throughout my working day. I'm experiencing them as the people they are, as gifted, resourceful, responsible people, who want to share with others in this enterprise. To the extent that that happens I'm much closer to experiencing men and women as what we are made to be: human projections of the faithful and responsibly creative God.

90

The owner of a furniture factory was recently asked why his firm was so successful. The reason, he said, was that 'around here the employees act as if they own the place'. He had given his employees a real sense of 'participation and ownership' in that business enterprise (Max De Pree).

A lot of firms already claim that – often without much basis. But in that furniture factory the employees do play a real part as persons. If they've worked there a year they have shares; they are kept informed about productivity and profits; their suggestions for improvement are welcomed and, if successful, rewarded. Above all they're *encouraged* to have a say in how they do their job and in how the firm is run. They are no longer just cogs, but the main engine.

It is good to be able to look around in your office or factory and see not automatons but lively, resourceful people working with you towards a shared enterprise that you all believe in. It is good to see the people with you working not just for the money but because their self-respect is tied up in it: it has become for them an expression of their gifts and their personality and of a solidarity with this team. The human relations director of Thorn EMI summed up what you see when such 'participation' really happens. You find it enables 'people to take up the maximum space within themselves as individuals, not just within the organization. It is important to encourage people to bring all of themselves to work.' A long way indeed from Bill's supermarket!

That's no consolation to Bill. And, so far, relatively few people work in more progressive firms. So is that human kind of work out of reach for most of us?

If we were to push for it, we'd find to a large extent we were pushing an open door. In 1988 a survey of 250 British directors found they had 'an undoubted appreciation of the impact of employee involvement on business success'. Last week a former chairman of a major construction company told me 'It's simply common-sense'.

Most employers know that the current workforce is no longer like their fathers or grandfathers, most of whom left school at 14, and whose models of organization tended to be the old-style army. They know that a leading business consultant was right when he said that 'people now . . . expect to be consulted; to be listened to; to be informed; to be kept in the picture. Good leaders create that sense of being a team, of involvement and commitment' (John Adair).

Employers also know that employment has become, for the

91

skilled, a seller's market. Because of the low birthrate in the 1960s and 1970s there is a dearth of skilled workers. A skilled worker can therefore quite often choose a firm that offers a human kind of work-setting rather than one that does not. Employers are well aware that these workers often do.

Most employers would therefore agree with an *Independent* editorial that 'traditional approaches are no longer seen as adequate' and that 'active collaboration and involvement' is the key resource.

The reason why the door is only *partly* open is that employers see other things as well. In such a sensitive and crucial matter as dealing with people, it takes courage and confidence to change your ways. Middle management often feels threatened, because if those below them have both the information and the responsibility what role is left to them? A trade union can feel threatened, if confrontation is its method and collaboration is replacing it, or if changes may mean loss of jobs. Some of the workforce themselves may prefer the more autocratic ways that they've long been accustomed to. And won't listening to all these people take up valuable time? But the effort may be worthwhile in spite of difficulties.

The remarkable situation that now confronts us Christians is that the major activity of most people could be transformed into something much more human. There has never been a time when we could contribute so much to such a deep and wide enrichment. That will require skill and perseverance, but we would not expect otherwise.

The ultimate depth of any genuinely human action is God's Spirit working in us. When we act true to our humanity our life has a transcendence, a significance, that is beyond our powers to fathom. That transcendence is not a vague glow that hovers above our actions. Parents who have made sacrifices for their child can find it in the quality of themselves and their relationships as they become more fully human: the deepest joy and satisfaction, in spite of the further challenges it brings.

That transcendence is also found when we go beyond our own self-interest to help create a human kind of collaboration and creativity at work. We see people taking up 'a maximum space within themselves'. They have daily experience of making some part of this world good, in the service or the product, and in some of the inter-relationships. Scripture and Christian experience help us see that such a thing is part of a story whose scope and depth transcends our present limited vision, when men and women's vocation to share in

God's creativity is being implemented in these humdrum actions.

In the rest of this Part we shall review the tools which firms are using to make the work experience of their employees more human, so that the reader can consider the tools which are or could be used in his or her firm and what improvements should be sought. Prayer notes will offer a way to recognize something of the depth of what is being considered in each section.

At the end of the Part we shall reflect on how the churches could help.

Reflection

- To prepare yourself to consider the tools, you may like to reflect on your experience of jobs:
  - where the employees have been treated as cogs in a machine;
  - where there has been at least something of a 'family' context, and where people's personal contribution and need for love and fulfilment have been heeded.
- What difference did it make to the employees you knew well which of these approaches was the stronger? How did that affect:
  - trust?
  - motivation?
  - a feeling of care and concern for others?
  - a pride in the product or service?
- What mainly contributed to bringing about the second kind of work experience?
- As Christians we believe that God is found at the heart of life when there is love, responsible creativity and healing of relationships. Reflect on:
  - what Jesus' own life shows us about the full depth of this;
  - what picture Scripture gives us of the relationships and aims of a group of people influenced by God's Spirit (e.g. 1 Corinthians 13:4–7; 12:4–31; Galatians 5:22 – 6:2).
- Does real love for people involve our wanting them 'to take up the maximum space within themselves as individuals'? What helps people to take up that space as employees at work?

Eleven

Tools for the job

The kind of transformation of people's work we have been discussing can't be done by gimmicks. You are not just changing a few practices but the whole experience.

That was seen, for example, by BP Explorations in 1990. Instead of just issuing different procedures they announced six 'signposts' that together pointed to profound human values. The firm asked their entire workforce, at all levels, to follow the route where those signposts could take them: people, openness, teamwork, simplicity, trust and empowerment.

BP Explorations wanted something freer from bureaucracy, more flexible, with more scope for the workforce's gifts and initiatives, and where decision-making and responsibility were pushed further down the firm. They wanted the gifts and responsibility of their workforce to be unleashed. Those signposts would help people focus on the underlying values that could motivate them to choose that direction.

It is true that the tools we are about to look at are often used as gimmicks. They may be applied half-heartedly, to pretend there is participation. That may delude the shareholders but it won't delude the workforce. The real test, therefore, is not *whether* they are used but *why*. The role of Christians in all this becomes increasingly obvious.

Tool 1 Keeping the workforce in the picture

Larger firms

You can't feel part of a complex enterprise like a business if you're not regularly informed about what's going on. Over the 1980s, companies quickly began to realize that. A 1988 survey showed that over three-quarters of the companies surveyed had regular communication with their staffs. The proportion had nearly doubled over the last five years.

The difficulty, however, is that you can't get humanity on the cheap. The price of communication is not just the time it takes. It may also require us to revise our basic assumptions about ourselves and others, for instance that management is superior and the rest are not much more than tools. Jack, the factory manager of a large food firm near Manchester, pointed, from long experience, to the kind of road you have to take.

Jack's factory employs 1500 people on this site. 'Our survival depends', Jack told me, 'on the quality of our product and our service.' The key to success, he said, is in the senior management, including himself, 'visiting our people and communicating with them in a very consistent way. We feel that if we do that properly, involving our people, involving their input and ideas, all these other issues will be taken care of, because our people will feel right in the job they're doing.'

Much of that you could hear from many a chief executive. He or she might point with satisfaction to the firm's Mission Statement and to 'splendid' occasional staff meetings. How easily executives can deceive themselves about this was shown by a 1990 survey which found that most company communications strategies are poor and don't serve their declared purpose. They are based, the survey found, on 'military-type models', where officers (who are thought 'superior') dispense occasional information to the troops (who are thought 'inferior'). The result, not surprisingly, was found to be 'minimal employee commitment'.

Jack has no time for that kind of communication. His aim isn't to dish out bits of information but to 'get people to feel a real part of our business'. And the key to that, he finds, is for him and the department managers to walk around, every day, talking to people, going round the shop floor, finding out what their problems are, whether they're business- or home-related. He sees part of his job as making sure that the department managers never get too busy to spend time with their staff.

True, this isn't yet the communication of ideas for new policy, new equipment, and the company's financial situation and prospects. But what it is doing is laying the necessary foundation for that so that the workforce feels that those are 'our' concerns, not just 'theirs'.

My conversations with this firm's employees and with local people certainly suggested that that was happening in Jack's company. Employees in other firms envied those who worked there.

On to this walk-around practice Jack builds other methods. He has hired a counsellor to whom staff can go, if they wish, to talk through confidential problems. In addition, Jack's door is always open for anyone who wants a private conversation, and so is his deputy's. This is partly to cater for those who are less happy with the informal approach. 'I want these people to know that I'm one of them. We're all the same together. And I want them to be involved in activities such as decision-making.'

With this foundation in place, occasional general meetings become worthwhile. Through this regular informal footwork of Jack and the department managers the employees know the business, feel they are known and valued as colleagues, and therefore feel involved.

So, was Jack complacent about what he and his managers were achieving? 'If we don't listen to our employees', he told me as I was leaving, 'as to how they'd like to be communicated with, and continue to improve our communication, I'll guarantee we'll fail.'

Smaller firms

A good smaller firm will also keep employees in the picture, by similar methods, but they'll be handled more informally.

A danger is that the easier relationships by themselves may be wrongly taken by the employer as proof that the employees do feel they are being kept in the picture. To avoid that danger, a wise employer will perhaps make a 'shopping list' of objectives similar to Jack's and ensure that they are achieved in ways that suit that firm's size and character.

Whatever the size of the firm, a key strategy is the one that Jack implied at the end of our interview. His firm regularly reminds its employees that it wants continually to improve its communication with them. Even in a small firm the employees may feel that there aren't enough of either formal or informal sessions.

What might be done?

For all in the firm

- What do you think of Jack's key to success: 'our people feeling right in the job they're doing'?
- What more could you do to help your colleagues feel that?
- What could others, including management, do? And what could you do to encourage them to do it?

For people in senior management

- Is keeping employees 'in the picture' optional for a Christian?
- What informal and formal steps could you take to improve this in your firm?

Prayer-notes

Experience Reflect on examples of employers keeping their employees in the picture and of any of us helping people feel right in the job they're doing.

Pointers-to-depth For St Paul, 'love is building people up' (1 Corinthians 8:1). In his own work, 'Everything we do, dear friends, is done to build you up' (2 Corinthians 12:19). A Christian group of people does that very practically: 'Love one another warmly . . . show respect to one another . . . Let your hope keep you joyful . . . share your belongings . . . open your home to strangers . . . be happy with those who are happy, weep with those who weep. Have the same concern for everyone' (Romans 12:10–16).

Response What action could you take to promote a good use of this tool in your work situation?

Tool 2 Valuing employees' experience and ideas

The president of a company was once asked what he thought limited the success of most companies. His answer was 'The fact that people further down the ladder always consider themselves less valuable or creative human beings'.

In both large and small firms, managers who regularly show interest and friendship with the workforce and keep them regularly in the picture are beginning to change that. But, in addition, they must want the employees to be involved, so far as possible, in activities like decision-making. Shortly before my last visit, Jack's firm had needed to buy equipment. The management had thoroughly consulted all those who would be associated with that equipment. 'We want them to be a true part of everything that's going on here', was Jack's explanation. And, of course, such consultation would be likely to lead to a better choice.

Adequately applying this tool involves much more than just the occasional consultation on such things as new equipment. We see this when we turn to what happened in a Liverpool firm, staffed by forty people and making one product. Even in that small firm there were strong tensions between sections, particularly between maintenance and production. The (not unusual) macho attitude to management meant that its leadership was viewed mainly negatively. All this led to a weak motivation to work well or in close collaboration with colleagues.

The factory manager saw the problem, and also the solution. First, he showed that management was strongly committed to listening. On that he built a leadership style that was more about sharing agreed aims and targets than about issuing precise demands.

This gradually led to a huge change in attitudes in that factory. While work had consisted just of responding – or not! – to precise demands, most people had worked half-heartedly, with indifference or resentment about the work-interests of other sections. Now, working together on aims and targets was beginning to bring them together as a team. 'These are the things we've got to achieve. I can do that. We can increase the speed of this machine. If you can do that, and I can do that, between us we can do that.'

When the manager described this to me, he realized that it sounded too good to be true. 'All I can say', he said, 'is that I saw it happen.'

To achieve it you have to opt firmly for the listening approach, but you've also got to give that a certain amount of structure. Every Friday morning the representatives of each department meet to look together at the top four problems of that week and how together they will try to solve them. 'When that happens', said the manager, 'you start to realize that $2 + 2$ can equal $4\frac{1}{2}$.'

In a larger firm this would still be possible if there were a strong clarity of purpose. A first step towards that is often a 'suggestions scheme'. If such a scheme is run well it will be telling people all the way down the ladder that the company values their experience, their responsibility and their thinking. Often this will be reinforced by giving financial rewards for suggestions that lead to savings or to increased productivity. In 1989 the Industrial Society found that 'many large companies are each saving £1 million a year as a result of the suggestions, and some employees were receiving substantial rewards for their ideas'.

Obviously suggestion schemes, like briefings, can be just lip-service to collaboration. The management must actually believe and acknowledge that junior staff can produce better ideas than them. Otherwise the limitations that president pointed to will remain as strong as before. But such an acknowledgement is not easy for a manager who may well be feeling insecure, in rapidly changing and very competitive times.

If the staff are not convinced that management really welcome upwards communication in all aspects of the business, then suggestion scheme meetings often make poor management–staff relations worse. The meetings tend to become more an excuse to voice criticism of management – a letting off steam! – than a means for making constructive suggestions for improvements, which it is felt would be wasted anyway.

But if the staff *have* been convinced that their ideas are genuinely valued, then sharing in forming them and working them out increases their feeling of solidarity both with management and among themselves. They feel valued team-mates in a common task. The same would of course happen in a smaller firm.

On what kind of topics should suggestions be welcomed? The most obvious topics are the details of the day-to-day organization and running. The employees' daily experience of that obviously qualifies them to suggest improvements. This possibility encourages them to act as resourceful problem-solvers, instead of just followers of a routine.

It's equally important to involve the employees in deciding about the issues at the other end of the spectrum, especially the overall aim of the company. Significantly, business consultants usually call that the company's 'vision'. There is more in any genuinely human enterprise than what can be measured in terms of money.

There is a need to take seriously targets like people, teamwork and empowerment. What companies are finding is that without such depth as part of the aim, there is inadequate motivation for many to give their best to the company.

Awareness of that fact is spreading. People are aware of outstanding success stories like that of the firm where the workforce helped management to form a strong vision and a business plan to match. Within a year the company had increased its revenue by 60 per cent and more than doubled the number of its clients.

Handling a suggestion scheme for such a purpose naturally requires certain skills. If the chief executive has never learnt to do much more than manage the system, then handling a discussion of values could prove difficult without further training. In a 1989 study of 1,500 senior executives, the trait most frequently described as important for a leader for the year 2000 was an ability to convey a strong sense of vision. But, for years, plenty of firms will be stuck with bosses who see no need to pick up that skill, or may be not have the ability to pick it up.

This is small consolation to any of us if our company is stuck with a leader of that kind. And even if our leader *is* endowed with vision, we still have to view any vision critically. It can be a vision that is constricting or shallow or dishonest. Even so, it can be to our great advantage to keep the need for a healthy vision and a leader who can handle that as at least a long-term goal. When the opportunity eventually arises, such leadership can transmute our work experience.

What might be done?

Employers Most employers understand these developments but also see difficulties:

1. Any business has to get right a complex web if it is going to survive: capital, profits, sales, public image, wages, staff and everyday administration. Would a fully-developed suggestion scheme force me to adopt policies that would seriously damage that web? Would it force me to divulge to staff information that could give our rivals an advantage?
2. If I'm more a manager than a leader and haven't had training in leadership skills, dare I risk introducing a suggestion scheme?

- Could some people in senior management get together on a regular basis and share some of their experience of these issues? Could you hear employers who have overcome these difficulties and judge whether you could apply similar solutions?
- Whatever decisions you take on that, could you consider the level of trust you give to your staff? Could you entrust the staff with 'the whole picture', training them where necessary to interpret accounts and the firm's financial and other policies?

- Could you trust the staff to understand that no one is an ideal leader and management may need to acquire more leadership skills? Would such an admission create greater solidarity and trust?

Employees
- Could you help, when necessary, to overcome what can be one of the greatest obstacles to good relationships between employer and employees: employees insisting, against any realism, that a boss should be ideal?
- Could you reflect more on our Christian insight that our human vocation is to be co-creative in a *flawed* human world, and to share in God's strongest characteristic of loving compassion for people's neediness and weakness?
- Although it is hard to share in that approach when you are a victim of waste and even injustice, could you try more to see flaws in your leader from God's perspective, and also to value the service he or she should perform for this organization?
- Since effective suggestion schemes increase the atmosphere of collaboration in a firm, what could you do that would
  - lead to such a scheme being introduced (if it hasn't been already)?
  - help it foster trust, involvement, and collaboration in the firm?

Prayer notes
Experience Reflect on the difference it has made (or might make) to your feelings about your involvement in some activity at work or elsewhere to have your experience and ideas valued in setting the methods, aims and targets.

Pointers-to-depth How may we
- join in God's work of overcoming the divisive forces like racism, sexism and class that prevent us living as kin with each other (e.g. Galatians 3:27–28)?
- live as a 'body' where each member honours the gifts, and delights in the achievements of, the other members (1 Corinthians 12)?

Response
- Act and speak confidently as a member.
- Seek to value colleagues more.

- Act to promote a good use of this tool in your work situation.
- Thank God for having a part in God's work of helping us find true human kinship.

Tool 3 Encouraging employees to develop their skills

We've seen how employees may be encouraged to contribute their ideas and suggestions. But even more fundamental is, of course, the everyday application of the skills people have been hired for. How can that central element of work be made more humanly fulfilling?

I shall need to feel that my firm values my skills because they are an important part of me *as a person*, not just as an employee. And in this age, when technology and techniques so rapidly become obsolete, I won't feel that unless the firm is interested in the *development* of my skills.

The method firms use for showing interest in employees' skills is regular appraisal. In the right hands (which are likely to need some training for this) appraisals become regular opportunities for the employee to sit down with his or her manager and work out together the employee's attainable objectives in the context of the business's objectives and his or her skills and aspirations.

A well-conducted appraisal focuses on strengths and achievements more than on weaknesses and helps the employee do better at what he or she already *wants* to do: use these skills and this experience to contribute. Because the aspirations of the employee are part of the context, the appraisal will raise such questions as, What role would the employee eventually like to have and what could be done, over the next few years, to develop the skills needed for that role? In a smaller firm this could be a severe test of the firm's real concern for a valued employee, since through encouraging such development it could eventually lose a valued asset.

A good appraisal also enables difficulties to be tackled sympathetically and constructively. If the appraisal is agreed by both parties, the weaknesses shown up are problems that both understand and wish to tackle. If the employee disagrees with any criticism, then he or she records dissent. Most appraisal schemes give employees the opportunity to read their report and to record any dissent.

Through all these means, a process that could be threatening or even destructive becomes one that is generally appreciated by both the employee and the firm.

What might be done?
People in senior management
- Although you know that an appraisal scheme can offer a great service to the employees – and very probably to the firm itself – you also know that it needs to be applied sensitively and humanely, that it probably involves the cost of training, and that it gives an extra task to some of the abler managers. Even so, could you take steps to ensure that a well-run appraisal scheme is in place, particularly for what it can offer to your employees?

Employees
- Since you know that even to remain in a job, it is often necessary to develop new skills, could you seek, or (if already in place) show your appreciation of, a good appraisal scheme in your firm *for others*, not just for yourself?

Prayer-notes
Experience Reflect on your experience of people you know well growing in personality and skills, and of your own contribution to such growth. Also reflect on the times when other people have helped you grow and of the difference that made to you.

Pointers-to-depth 'God gives ability to everyone for their particular service. The Spirit's presence is shown in some way in each person for the good of all' (1 Corinthians 12:6–7).
'Who made you superior to others? Didn't God give you everything you have?' (1 Corinthians 4:7).
'I came that you might have life, and have it more abundantly' (John 10:10).
'Everything we do, my own dear people, is to build you up' (2 Corinthians 12:19).

Response Thank God that his kindness is shown in every person in their ability for their particular service (*charis-ma* = being given God's kindness).
What could you do to help people at work and elsewhere to develop their skills 'for their particular service'?

Tool 4 Mentoring

Mentoring focuses more directly on your developing your career.

At present it is normally used to help junior managers find a quicker route up the career ladder by providing them with an older person within the firm who will give them advice, friendship and support. This helps the younger managers feel that the company values them; it gives them confidence, contacts, access to a lot of experience and a better idea of their own potential and limitations.

The advantages to the company are also considerable, especially in improving the quality of its senior management.

Mentoring can also be used to help disadvantaged groups, like women and ethnic groups, improve their career opportunities. This kind of use is so far much less common but successful examples are known.

What might be done
For all in the firm

- Could the more experienced people in the firm show a willingness to offer those who may need it a helping hand with their careers if asked to do so?
- Could a mentoring scheme be considered for those groups it might help?

Prayer-notes
As for Tool 3 above.

Tool 5 Counselling

If you are going to help make work more human, the way the workplace is organized cannot be the only factor you have to deal with. A major factor will be people's personal circumstances.

If I am worried sick about my teenage son or daughter, or my marriage, or a debt I can't pay, then I am far less likely to care about the firm's aims and how to attain them. If I have serious alcohol or drug problems, I shall feel even less involved.

Unfortunately difficulties like these aren't only for the few. In the USA, in some urban areas, three out of four marriages end in divorce and 10 per cent of the workforce have alcohol or drug problems. A million British people have long-term dependence on drugs, and a recent survey of British chief executives found widespread 'tension' problems.

The personal problems that limit people's work experience mainly originate outside the workplace: things like strain from family relationships, emotional difficulties, money problems, drugs and alcohol.

The kind of help many need can be illustrated by an experience of my friend, Derek. 'When I was a factory manager', Derek told me, 'one of the supervisors of one of the departments flopped down in my office and said "I have a problem". I listened. He talked for three-quarters of an hour. Then he went away saying "You've been a great help". I'd only listened. But he was visibly much better.'

All Derek had done was provide the listening ear. Many people have no friend, spouse, minister or priest whom they feel they can turn to. That is what a counselling service provides, and firms are becoming aware of the importance of providing such a service.

Since introducing one, the Post Office has seen a reduction in staff turnover and absenteeism. In an American firm, in 1985, the counselling programme for alcohol and drugs alone saved it a million dollars in lost working days for the 310 employees who benefited from such counselling. However, recent British research shows that 'Many companies are failing to respond to their employees' human needs . . . such as counselling, child-care and policies designed to reduce the conflict between family and working life' (Dr Tony Munton, Sheffield University).

A friend who has run two factories told me what those companies are missing. 'There is a great deal of harmony, energy, drive that can come about in an organization where the word really does get around that if you've got a problem you really can talk about it. It tends to provoke very positive feelings.' The smaller firm would find it difficult to provide an in-house counsellor, but there is an organization with the appropriate initials EAR which can provide a firm with a very professional service.

A Christian counsellor in a large firm told me what his job feels like to him. 'It's tiring, it's unbelievably tiring. But fascinating. There's often a sense of hopelessness. That's where my faith is important.' His main experience of his job was very positive. 'You get this unbelievable wisdom coming out from these people who have struggled or are struggling. This incredible goodness. This mutual support. This help they're getting from God. They're wonderful people.'

This counsellor's experience had convinced him that by providing a counselling service a firm reduces suffering, releases energy and commitment, and makes the firm more profitable. And, 'as the word gets round, it tends to provoke very positive feelings about the organization'.

What might be done
For all at work

- Are there some people in the firm whom you sometimes help at critical times by providing a listening ear which they might not otherwise get?
- Could you take a greater interest in the personal welfare of your workmates?
- Could you discuss the advantages to individuals and to the firm of having some counselling service, whether in-house or not?

For people in senior management

- Could managers be given some basic counselling skills so that they become better at being sensitive to the burdens that a large proportion of most workforces carry?

Prayer-notes
Experience When has a listening ear meant a lot to you? Does your experience of yourself and/or of people you know well suggest that a substantial number of people bring problems to their workplace that can damage them and their work?

Pointers-to-depth 'The son of man came to serve' (Mark 10:45).
'Love builds up' (1 Corinthians 8:1).
'Everything we do, dear friends, is done to build you up' (2 Corinthians 12:19).

> I ask God from the wealth of his glory
> to give you power through his Spirit to be strong in your
>   inner selves,
> and I pray that Christ will make his home in your hearts
>   through faith.
> I pray that you may have your roots and foundation in love,
> so that you, together with all God's people,
> may have the power to understand how broad and long,
> how high and deep,

is Christ's love.
(Ephesians 3:16–18)

Response Among the stresses and problems many of us have to face today, what could you do to help some of those you work with?

Tool 6 Having a stake in the enterprise

We work for a wage, and a company must operate profitably. How does money affect our experience of work?

We are all familiar with the *negative* effects money can have when you feel your wage is too low, or that the wages of others are too high, or if you believe the firm is making an unfair profit, say at the expense of Third World countries or other consumers.

Among the *positive* effects money can have is through employees owning shares. Such ownership is likely to strengthen the employee's feeling of involvement in the enterprise and therefore to diminish the Us–Them divide. It also makes the company more profitable, through the feeling of greater involvement and through making the workforce more profit-conscious and readier to take long-term views about the company. Recent legislation in Britain has made it much easier for companies to have employee share-ownership plans.

But that greater involvement occurs only if the share-ownership accompanies the other means of employee involvement we have been considering. It is those means, not share-ownership by itself, that are found to be determinative.

This confirms what we know from other surveys, that the pay, although usually essential, isn't the main satisfaction people need from their work. That satisfaction comes only from work being a genuinely human experience.

What might be done
For all in the firm
- Could you check that your firm keeps under review ways in which all employees could have a financial stake in the enterprise, if it hasn't such a scheme already?
- If your firm hasn't yet considered such a scheme, could the experience of comparable firms that do have a scheme be discussed?

The church's contribution

Michael is a Christian businessman who has run a widely admired engineering firm for thirty years. When he read a draft of this chapter his chief comment was on the need for the church's contribution to the developments we have been considering.

These tools, he agreed, are ways of 'trying to get a better deal in terms of everybody fulfilling themselves. That doesn't mean that just the workplace benefits from it, but also the whole society.'

Since Michael's own firm began to use these tools forty years ago, he can speak with some authority about this. The chief barrier, he finds, is the fact that businesses cannot develop a more human culture in isolation, and no forum exists in which they can hammer one out together.

'Is this not where the Christian churches', he asked, 'have a vital role to play? Can they not become meeting places where employers and employees can discuss, not the technical and commercial concerns within their particular enterprises, but the more basic and universal concerns – motivation, fulfilment, trust and confidence, care and concern – all the things that go to make up a culture?'

Michael saw this as 'central to the Christian churches as we approach the twenty-first century'. Our first Part showed that this should be the case because of the church's very purpose.

To begin to achieve this, the local churches of an area will probably want to embark on a process in which all their members can take the perspectives discussed in Part One on board. As the process helps their members do that, they will feel able to seek out local businesses and other organizations in the area that would like a more human culture.

Success will partly depend on the churches' conviction that God's good news is not confined to regular worshippers. Out of that conviction they will become listening churches, respectful of and grateful for the goodness and wisdom they see in others.

Obviously much of the life of an area happens outside its paid work organizations. The values of love, kinship, healing and human fulfilment must also be fostered in those other spheres, like parenting, the lives of the retired and in coping with social problems. The opportunities in those spheres are discussed in other parts of this book.

The great Christian insight is that at the centre of *all* there is good news. Jesus calls it God's transforming power or 'Kingdom'; Paul calls it God's creative power ('Spirit') or gracious kindness. It is a yeast that leavens the dough, it is the rock on which we find complete security, the seed that grows to harvest. It is also a work that we find our true selves in taking our part in.

PART FOUR
RETIRED PEOPLE

Twelve

The Age of Living

For years, my cousin Dot travelled every summer from her home in the north of Scotland to the south of France for her holiday. Then one year she decided she was too old and just went to Cornwall instead. She was 91!

Most of us know retired people as lively as Dot. I think of my friend Alan who went off to Africa at the age of 77, 'because I haven't explored that civilization yet', or my aunt who insisted on going on a pilgrimage to the Holy Land at 84.

People like that force us to revise our ideas about what our sixties and seventies can be like. They open our eyes to facts that we hadn't much noticed.

The most obvious one is the *length* of the retirement stage of our lives. While a hundred years ago life ended, on average, at about 45, now 77 per cent of women and 64 per cent of men are still alive at 70, often with reasonable health and further years to come.

But the main good news about the retirement years is less their number than the *quality* of life we can have in them. Unfortunately, most of us are being cheated of this good news by the image we have inherited of retirement as a rapid decline into inactivity and poor health. In the 1990s that image is being changed by our realization that only 4 per cent of those above retirement age claim they are in very poor health. Up to now, retirement has tended to be, for most people, like owning a powerful sports car and using it just for some local shopping. Today, as never before, all that could change.

To see the contribution we could make as Christians to that change, we need to recall the opportunities that retirement offers most people and the barriers that can stand in the way of people taking them.

What happens when we retire? The likelihood is that for the first time in our lives we have the leisure and freedom to do what we really want, with that decision based on mature experience and wisdom. It is what a retired hospital worker called 'the transition from one who had been a person to whom life happened to someone who makes choices' (Jean Sealey, *The Listener*, 14 June 1990). No wonder the French call this period 'The Age of Living'. It is when we can engage in the activity which really fits our personality and gives us a sense of fulfilment.

But when we retire, do we in fact take up new ideas, studies or hobbies, or do we embark on voluntary action? Probably most of us find that that is the exception rather than the rule.

One of the barriers to our making the most of our new freedom is the stereotype we have already noticed of retirement being an age of inactivity. The extent of the lost energy may be suggested by one American city where it was found that 44 per cent of those in their sixties and seventies were potential volunteers or employees, if transport, expenses and the work-schedules were right.

A second barrier to our making this the Age of Living is poverty. In 1991, a third of senior citizens in Britain had to cope on a weekly income of under £88 per household, and over one and a half million were living officially at the poverty level. When you have severe worry about money, and no spare money for developing your interests, you are unlikely to regard your retirement as the Age of Living! The very idea is 'a mockery of the poorer old, who have been and lamentably still are, so large a proportion in retirement' (Peter Laslett).

The third barrier is that we are not offered appropriate counselling, especially in the years before retirement. Even if I do realize that there probably stretch before me many years, after my retirement, when I could take up an interest I would find deeply fulfilling, it may well not be clear to me which of the many possible interests would suit me best or what options are available. The actual year of retirement can be a bad time to consider all this, since giving up a job is often a wrench, and there can be other changes as well to contend with. A good counsellor, some years beforehand, can help us find the path that suits us best. Then, when retirement comes, we are eager and ready to take up the interest strongly. It is known that most people would welcome such help. Unfortunately, at present, very little of it is offered.

If we Christians are going to be good news, then overcoming the barriers of stereotyping, of poverty among the elderly, and of lack of counselling must be central aims of ours for the ten million retired people in our country. Reflecting on Scripture has made it possible for us to see that to show Christian love of our neighbour is to share in the whole task of making people's lives more human. We therefore should think of what we could do, both as citizens with votes and as local people and members of our church, to find ways in which:

- the opportunities of this Age of Living can be more widely recognized;
- planning and counselling can be made more available to help us make much more of this age;
- the poverty of a high proportion of retired people can be overcome;
- education, which in Britain is at present thought of as almost entirely for the young, can be made more available to retired people.

Paid work for the retired

In this area, too, the life of older people could be much improved if we really wanted that to happen. The quality of life of many of those of us who are retired would be much improved if more employers and Jobcentre staffs could overcome prejudice against older workers. A quarter of retired people are interested in returning to paid work, but most of them believe they will not find a job as employers only want to employ younger people. The difficulties of older people who want to work are further compounded by the fact that they are often denied training opportunities. Yet 'Older people should be ideal targets for corporate recruiters everywhere', said *The Economist*: 'They are less likely to miss work, more polite to customers, and more loyal than their younger counterparts' (6 January 1990). This was amply confirmed by a DIY store that adopted such a policy. The firm now hires only those of 50 or older for its sales staff, and their average age is 57. Before, the store had difficulties, especially with staff turnover. Now it is 18 per cent more profitable than comparable stores, and absenteeism and staff turnover are both much improved. The chain the store belongs to, B & Q, is so pleased with the result that it wants to have 10 per cent of its national workforce 50 or over (*The Independent*, 2 October 1991). In Germany two-thirds of companies employ pensioners part time.

A helpful factor is a political consensus that seems to be emerging in favour of a flexible retirement policy. Very likely such a policy should consist of giving those between 60 and 70 a choice, throughout those years, of working full time or part time, or drawing an adequate pension.

Dependent old people

As people become older, there is obviously an increasing number of things they cannot do for themselves, like heavy gardening and repair work. Living alone, and restricted mobility, can lead to a feeling of isolation. Yet half the retired people in a recent survey said that they required no extra care or attention as they grew older. Most retired people are proudly self-sufficient and feel supported by family, friends or neighbours.

Even so, there is obviously a large number who, in varying degrees, are dependent on others for their quality of life or even to be able to continue living in their own home. There are few more haunting images for any of us than a helpless and abandoned old person. In fact a huge number of people do share in the work of caring for those who are dependent. One could point to the quarter of a million volunteers who help Age Concern in their 1,400 organizations round the country, as well as the work of many churches and synagogues.

The carers
This large group of people are some of our country's most unsung heroes. There are more than 300,000 single people caring for an elderly relative in their home, and at least a third of elderly people will be carers at some point in their retirement. 'Loneliness and exhaustion are the most common problems facing carers. Society takes them for granted and leaves them to cope alone' (Frank Glendenning). Even many social workers are unaware of the importance of help given by carers.

114

We could think of a daughter looking after her demented mother for several years, or of my friend Jane, the head of a comprehensive school, who looks after her increasingly housebound 90-year-old mother. In spite of her very demanding job, Jane can have hardly any social life, and even a week's holiday once or twice a year depends on whether someone can be found at the right moment whom her mother feels at ease with and who can look after her while Jane takes her holiday.

What these carers are doing is giving a dependent person what he or she values so much: the ability to lead a relatively independent life in their own homes for as long as possible.

Another form of care that many of us are involved in is good neighbourliness. In any locality there are many people who are prepared to give help to a neighbour in need. The churches are known to be the foremost promoters of neighbourhood care schemes.

When you link both these types of care with the services the local authorities provide, like Meals on Wheels and Home Helps, and the services provided by voluntary organizations like Age Concern, then you have a rich partnership. That partnership could boast of the fact that only 3 per cent of those over 65 have to live in institutions, with the average age of a new resident being about 82. When we get together on these things, it is astonishing and heartening what can be achieved!

Some of the needs of dependent old people can be tackled best by working through organizations like Age Concern, with its expertise and resources. Most of us know people to whom it is – or could be – a godsend to have access to a day centre where a dependent person can have a hot meal, a social life and access to educational opportunities and outings. Through its volunteers Age Concern tries to provide such centres around the country. In addition, there are those who will have to leave their home for an institution if they cannot get bathing and personal attention. Through voluntary work in a day care centre, we can help people stay in their homes.

Another common situation we can help with is panic about money. Most of those over 75 live alone, with a severe lack of money; although they are entitled to several benefits from the state, many do not know how to apply for them. Resource workers visit them to advise them and often prevent much worry.

Retired people are good news

A huge number of families with young children would obviously agree with that! Many mothers could not get to work without the help of a grandparent. Every family could make its own list of what it owes the older generation.

As we increasingly recognize retirement as the Age of Living, we appreciate better other reasons why retired people are good news. When we retire we have behind us much experience and our own skills, with more time and freedom than the younger generations have. With a bit of encouragement and perhaps counselling to get us going, there is obviously much that we could do to help transform people's lives in our locality, or even beyond.

Of course the range of options is much wider than helping fellow retired people. But it is worth recalling that in the 1,400 local Age Concern organizations, most of the volunteers are themselves retired people. The volunteers may take up social visiting of the isolated or give practical help. Retired people who have been trained in counselling could be valuable for a counselling service to help people plan for their retirement.

What might we do
For all of us
- How could we encourage both younger and older people to recognize better that retirement can be for most of us the Age of Living?
- What effect should our realization of this opportunity have on:
  - how we plan our retirement;
  - our mainly unspoken assessments of older people's capacities;
  - our efforts, whether in lobbying or through local initiatives, to enable these years to be for most elderly people years of fulfilment? For example, we might help to overcome the lack of counselling facilities for planning retirement; lobby politicians to tackle the poverty that at present afflicts a huge number of the elderly; show our support for the carers by helping with the heavier chores, offering some companionship, or sometimes standing in for them (two-thirds of them receive no help, and many are not in good health); take part in a neighbourhood care scheme.

For those who are elderly
- How are *you* being good news to those you live among?
- What needs are there in your neighbourhood which you could meet?
- How can you be good news to younger neighbours, relations, etc.?

For employers
- What could you do to enable older people who want a job which they are capable of doing to get work (e.g. by helping to overcome ageist stereotypes in your firm)?

For local churches
- What can we do to increase awareness among the members of our church and others of the opportunities and needs of older people?
- What can we do, as a local church, to initiate or to join in efforts like the ones listed above?
- What can older people do to contribute to our church's work and mission?

Prayer-notes
Experience Reflect on what you have done or would like to do to make the years of retirement for yourself or someone else the Age of Living.

Pointers-to-depth
> None of us lives for ourself only, None of us dies for ourself only.
> If we live, it is for the Lord we live, and if we die, it is for the Lord that we die.
> God's Kingdom is a matter of righteousness, peace, and joy, which the Spirit gives.
> So we must always aim at those things that bring peace and that help to strengthen one another.
> (Romans 13:7 – 14:20)

Response With regard to the elderly whom you know personally, or who live in your area, what more could you do that would 'aim at those things that bring peace and that help to strengthen one another'?

PART FIVE
BEING GOOD NEWS TO OUR NEIGHBOURS

Thirteen

Disabled people

Jack has the makings of an outstanding footballer. He has to choose whether to follow that career as someone concerned just with his success as an individual player or as someone really concerned with the team.

We know that it is the same with our other activities. Whether as a parent or as a worker, a player of some sport or a neighbour, do I try to find myself by just looking after my own interests or in human solidarity with others?

We were made to be kin. We find our true selves through exercising our human kinship, living in human solidarity with others because we recognize them as kin. Few can help us to do that more than disabled people.

Really becoming kin, as any family knows, involves taking on board two realities: each of us is a different 'member' of this body of people; and quite often that is tough because each of us is flawed.

Those realities are hard, especially of course the flaws. But when we get in deep touch with ourselves we know that a smooth ride, without the flaws, would make us characterless and unaware of the deep fulfilment to be found in depending on each other through unselfishness, tolerance and support. We need some degree of challenge, if only to feel our limitations, our sharing in the 'tough labour of love', and our wonder and need of God's enduring love and faithfulness.

Few speak that message more clearly to the rest of us than disabled people can if we allow them to. Mostly, perhaps, we don't allow them to.

Yes, we're kind to them, but isn't that often more as objects of our pity and less as essential partners in the enrichment of human life? To the extent that that is so, we fail to recognize *them* as persons, and we *ourselves* fail to act as persons in the real human world. Our chances of doing these things are much increased when we are habitually alongside disabled people, whether in our school, our work, or in our social lives.

In Britain we stand at a moment of great opportunity as regards disabled people. With the honourable exception of many individual carers and a handful of organizations, British society gave little attention to disabled people until recently. Even two decades ago, our social security system did not even treat them as a special category. Since then there have been considerable advances in our knowledge about their needs and in attempts to meet those needs. In the present decade we could take that much further. But the key to any full success will be the rediscovery of those perspectives about human kinship and co-creativity that we have found in Scripture. If we don't, we shall not be able to make a case in 'the constant tussle between the general electorate's broad sympathy for those who are worse-off and its reluctance to make itself worse-off in order to do something about it' (Gillian Dalley).

Disabled people

There are six and a half million people in the UK who are disabled, over two million of them in the categories of more severe disability; four million have mobility problems.

If I use a wheelchair, what might life look like?

I will probably have to go, at least at secondary stage, to a special school, where I shall be largely cut off from the stimulation and company of the rest of my age group. If this is the case for me, I will know that the main reason is that the other schools have buildings which have been constructed on the assumption that people like me can be reckoned 'outsiders'.

Again and again, buildings will give me that message. My friends may decide to go to a cinema, a meeting, a pub, or a course of lectures; while for me physical access can be difficult or impossible to the building itself, to lavatories and to other amenities.

With luck I will be aware that there is an increasing readiness today to avoid creating this problem. More than a decade ago research showed that 'disabled people perceive access difficulties as the most fundamental cause and manifestation of discrimination', and, as a result, an amendment to the Building Regulations obliges access to be considered in all new public buildings – though it doesn't at present apply to older buildings or to housing. 'A church would be the first to adopt that standpoint', I might assume. 'Since a church is primarily the members as the "body" of Christ, not just the building, surely it will make all its members welcome?'

In a growing number of churches I will find that is the case – though also in many churches, it has as yet hardly been considered. Some churches do make the building accessible to me by a ramp, but still show that they are not really set to welcome me. They may show that by treating me with patronizing kindness, so that I am much more an object than a person with gifts, experience and wisdom, or by not even noticing that meetings or lavatories are inaccessible to me. In those churches I know that I am still one of 'Them', while the rest are 'Us'. I realize that the members don't mean any unkindness. They are the victims of the assumption that 'We' don't have disabilities and that we who have are not an integral part of the local church's life. They have lost touch with the real humanity in which the Word 'came to dwell among us' (John 1:14 – literally, 'pitched his tent among us') and in which alone he can be found. To the extent that that happens, their Christianity has ceased to fulfil its real purpose and has degenerated into a soothing set of customs and notions.

Again with luck, I will have felt that I have resources, gifts and a part to play just as much as others. Recent developments may be helping to give me the reassurance about this that all of us need. While society catches up I will, in spite of many frustrations, take more confident joy in my human dignity and in the role that God, in his gracious kindness, has given me. People will still patronize me or avoid me, but it is easier to see now that that might be their loss more than mine.

Even so, when I leave school or further education to look for work, considerable difficulties may face me. Again I shall be glad about the promising trends. There is more government money for disabled people's training and employment services; and these are increasingly being offered in the mainstream, with everyone else, not segregated. Employers are beginning to get the point and to translate that into practice, but discrimination remains common, so that the average unemployment rate of disabled people is more than twice that of the rest.

If I want, I can find that there is a 'cafeteria' of measures that the State now offers to help us to get employment. I could put myself on the Disabled Persons Register or request a special kind of work situation or course tailored to my particular needs. But if I do get round to sorting out my opportunities, I'll be exceptional.

Part of the reason is morale. I am less likely to have qualifications – though 32 per cent of the current workforce do not have them either. Also, I know that many employers will not even consider employing a disabled person. Employment professionals know that these barriers could be overcome in much the same way as could those that face other unemployed people. The solution is to provide a counsellor to help us work out what we want and give us information and confidence; then to involve employers, so that their stereotypes of 'the disabled' are exposed to reality; and, finally, where necessary, to provide financial incentive for employers to take their share of disabled people into their workforce, as already happens in Germany but only to a very limited extent so far in Britain.

All this could be done if the will existed. Local authorities have in fact already been made responsible for providing counsellors (called Disabled Resettlement Officers). But, as we shall see, the service at present is very sketchy.

Perhaps the most promising fact of all is that the mindset *behind* some of the developments is more Christian. That German strategy takes on board the fact that, since we are all kin, disability is *everyone*'s business, not just the business of those with disabilities.

What might we do?

Elderly disabled people Most disabled people are over pension age, and so have already been talked about (see pages 111–17).

Poverty As we come to recognize the equal worth and dignity of disabled people, we increasingly find it unacceptable that, for example, 38 per cent of disabled male full-time employees – nearly three times the national average – have to live on less than £150 a week, especially given the fact that their disability is likely to involve them in extra expenses.

- Could I seek to move this fact higher up on the politicians' agenda?

Equal employment opportunities schemes
- Could I, if necessary, press my local authority to consider introducing an equal employment opportunities scheme? An increasing number of local authorities do tend to put on job advertisements. 'Applications from disabled people welcome', and then interview disabled people who apply and offer them, through the personnel officer, appropriate support.

Employers Although employers' earlier stereotypes of the work potential of disabled people are beginning to crumble, this process is still at an early stage. To a large degree people still think and say that disabled people are unemployable because 'they won't turn up on time; they're going to be a problem; and they're going to be off sick a lot'. An expert in this field told me 'If we can get people to think of disabled people correctly all the problems will in fact go away'. But until that happens many people will continue to be deprived of the opportunity of obtaining fulfilling, and often *any*, work. They will be unable to attain a decent standard of living for themselves and their families.

- Could a firm introduce some flexibility to adapt to a disabled person's circumstances? Getting to work on time every day, especially at rush hour, is difficult for some disabled people. In quite a range of jobs an employer could say: 'Work in the office two days a week; for the other three days, you could equally well work with a fax machine or telephone at home'.
- Could an employer let the disabled person go a quarter of an hour before the general factory exit, with all its rush?
- Could some of our local employers set a clear public standard in this matter for the rest of the locality, as employers like the BBC, British Telecom and British Gas are doing for the whole country?
- Could local employers and personnel officers in similar lines of business look together at this matter? If so, they could either call on appropriate local people to help them consider the actual needs and practical solutions, or they could turn to the Employers' Forum on Disability, set up by Business in the Community and the Prince of Wales Advisory Group to run courses and issue literature for this very purpose.

123

Employees

- Could you as an employee also be more flexible? An employee might say, for example, that a disabled fellow employee 'won't be able to lift the files, and I'm not going to do it for them'. But the disabled person might find it too cumbersome to go out to lunch and could mind the phone when no one else wants to do it, so that each helps the other.

Counselling Current research shows that many disabled people who seek jobs, and many who already have jobs, have a great need of career guidance. A good counsellor can help them steer through any rocks and shoals ahead, help them find openings and be helpful in enabling them to see more clearly their own talents and what work they would really like to have and could obtain.

Unfortunately research also shows that 'Very few people on Employment Training, including those with disabilities, appear to be getting the guidance they desperately need' (Stephen Pilling).

We have seen that local authorities have been charged to provide such a service through a Disablement Resettlement Officer who will see them and offer them an option on training programmes, contacts, or suggestions as to how they could perhaps continue their present employment within the bounds of their disability. But although some of them provide a good service, the lack of adequate resources and training makes that often not the case.

- Could the local churches in quite a wide area together set up a professional service of employment counselling for disabled people with regard to their employment, perhaps in partnership with the local officials, at least until a better public service can be created?

Carers There are nearly one and a half million principal carers to disabled people who need daily help. Recent research has shown that the support given to them is virtually non-existent. Three-quarters of these carers are relatives. A third of these are the only relative the disabled person has in their locality, so it is often difficult for the relative–carer to find someone who will regularly share the burden.

Local churches

- Could your local church invite the carers to meet from time to time and get to know each other? From such meetings carers could find ways of helping each other informally. Ways could also be found to offer a suitable 'relief-service' for those who need some time off, for shopping or for a respite. There may already be such a scheme in your area to which you could offer support or, perhaps with other local churches, you could consider setting up such a scheme.

- Could your local church search out and include disabled young people in church activities, youth clubs, Scouts and Guides, giving them a positive role, not just as on-lookers?
- Could you offer practical help (e.g. window cleaning, occasional paint washing, lawn mowing) to disabled parishioners? Respect for their independence would obviously be important, but members of a church can be available to give a practical boost when needed, in a non-patronizing manner.
- Could you see that large-print hymn books and service sheets are available? Also helpful would be a good public address system, warmth in church, and spaces within the congregation for wheelchairs so that disabled people do not have to be at the front or block the aisle.

Prayer-notes
Experience Reflect on occasions when you or others have lived and worked with disabled people as kin, not just as objects of kindness.

Pointers-to-depth
Let God transform you inwardly by a complete change of your
   basic attitudes.
We have many parts in the one body, and all these parts have
   different functions.
In the same way, though we are many, we are one body in
   union with Christ.
(Romans 12:2, 4–5)

Response In what ways could you respond more fully to the good news in disabled people?

Fourteen

Women at work

'You're girls, so of course you can't do this.' A tutor on a Youth Training Scheme was speaking recently to two girls on a course in heavy engineering. The fact that they were both very capable and had done well at metalwork at school didn't count for him. He made it such hell for them that eventually they left. His prejudice may have condemned them to an unfulfilling job for life.

Such stereotyping is the basic problem that women encounter at work. The others will be soluble once that has been cracked.

Largely because of such stereotyping, millions of women still suffer from low pay, low status, poor career prospects and little training. Many have to work far below the level to which their qualifications entitle them. Even in major companies where they may be 60 per cent of the workforce, they may hold only 1 or 2 per cent of the senior positions. Women hold less than 25 per cent of managerial jobs and comprise less than 5 per cent of directors. Yet the American guru on business leadership wrote in 1976 that 'women will make excellent managers' (Warren Bennis).

The churches must accept a degree of blame for the stereotyping. In any case, it is deeply ingrained in many men and many firms, and also in many women and their families. The fact that women are on average paid less than men reinforces it. 'You're paid less than others and you feel at the bottom of the pile' was how one woman expressed her feelings.

126

The worst damage is that it denies millions of women the fulfilment from their work that by nature we all need. It also robs the country of skilled workers that are greatly needed. And we are talking here about almost half of the workforce: 44 per cent now, and by the end of the century fully half.

Besides the damage done to women as individuals and to national productivity, there is something else as well. Mothering certainly gives women distinctive abilities. Genesis 2:21–25 seems to suggest that the most fruitful kind of activity is where male and female approaches do not exclude one another but are allowed to complement each other. Keeping most women 'at the bottom of the heap' diminishes the quality and effectiveness of many initiatives.

What do we need to do to prevent this impoverishment? There are three major barriers we need to dismantle.

Unequal pay

'Women's equality is still largely ignored at the pay-bargaining table' (Equal Opportunities Commission). This authoritative statement is borne out by well-known facts. Women's weekly earnings are on average 68 per cent of men's – the situation has hardly improved since 1983. A 1991 report found that discrimination in the workplace costs women more than £21 billion a year in pay. Is this a theft that sits easily on our consciences?

For families with a small mortgage and a working husband, this inequality may not hurt financially – though even there it can reinforce the assumption that women are less competent. But one in five families in Britain are single-parent, and in nine out of ten of them the single parent is the mother. In spite of having no help with the children from her husband, the woman will have to work, usually on an inadequate wage and with the day's timetable a constant shuttle. A recent television series found that 'there are many families with a single wage-earner where the income is too low to give children the start that society thinks they need' (*Breadline Britain*).

It would help to remove this obstacle if more pay negotiators were women (most at present are men) and if there were training in equality awareness for both management and unions. In other words, the main solution is to take practical steps to overcome the stereotypes.

Failure to provide for career needs of mothers

When women were regarded as 'extras' to the workforce in most types of work, it was easy to be unaware that there might be a problem. Now the need is obvious; and this country is just beginning to work out policies to deal with it. Adding to the urgency of tackling it is the considerable reduction in the number of school leavers this decade.

'We need a national co-ordinated child-care strategy', said the chair of the Equal Opportunities Commission. And in fact the 1990 Budget gave a tax break to employers who set up crèches at work, and a working group chaired by a government minister recommended child-care vouchers to enable more mothers to work. So perhaps the necessary momentum is beginning for the dismantling of this barrier?

At present very few firms have workplace nurseries or help employees to pay for child care. Since most feel that it costs too much to provide this for their employees, and for the smaller or medium-sized firm it is hardly practical, a system of vouchers would break the logjam. The vouchers could presumably be used near home: commuting to work with a baby has obvious difficulties!

Since only 15 per cent of women looking after children or elderly dependants want to return to full-time work, and a grandmother or a neighbour may be able to help them out, the lack of nurseries isn't the main problem with regard to most women's career break. To some working mothers without access to such help, child care is obviously an acute need, but for most the main need will be to find a way of picking up the threads of their career when they are ready to return. Here it should be possible for a firm to take some steps to help them. Although a firm cannot normally guarantee a place, it can encourage the mother to keep in touch with the firm and with the developments in her line of work. If it cannot itself offer her a job when she returns, it can at least listen for one on the grapevine. Some firms make the return of women easier by offering some job-sharing – though the administrative costs of that make it difficult for smaller firms.

The best solution in a locality might be a concerted effort from a range of organizations to help potential women returners discover the careers and opportunities open to them – as *Women's Hour*, with the Department of Employment and the Industrial Society, did in 1990. The organizers would have the satisfaction of providing more much-needed skilled workers for local business. What is the main motivation of employers to attract women back to work according to the Institute of Manpower? 'A growing recognition by employers that women are a vital skills resource.' They would also have the satisfaction of making a considerable contribution to these women's happiness, fulfilment and financial security.

Disadvantaged part-time work

A third of all working women, not far from five million, work part time. Their responsibilities, not just for young children but increasingly for elderly dependants, lead women to such employment. Often they have to change to part-time work at important stages of their careers.

Part-time employment has quite a poor image. Recent research has suggested that the disadvantages have been exaggerated. Also, part-time employees often have more freedom to do the job their own way than do full-time employees (Michael White).

But even when exaggerations are removed, White does still find serious disadvantages for many. One is the fact that there is seldom a pension – particularly serious for women forced into part-time work through being a single parent. Another is the lack of training and the absence of opportunities for promotion. As women increasingly achieve higher levels of education this is becoming intolerable to many. As a result, fewer are now willing to move into lower-level, part-time jobs after the birth of their children. Since employers mainly depend on women to fill those jobs, they may be forced to make changes.

Sexual harassment

Besides the injustices that largely arise from stereotyping, that of sexual harassment frequently degrades many women.

A woman may have to work in an office or factory where a suggestive calendar is displayed: perhaps one advertising cars by showing a woman as a mere sexual object rather than as a person.

Worse than that, naturally, is active sexual harassment: unwanted physical contact or sexual suggestions. This is particularly difficult to handle when it comes from a superior. Even in the more playful forms of 'You'll be all right, pet' kinds of conversation and bottom-pinching, or uninhibited behaviour at office parties, it degrades the relationship to a sub-personal level as well as making women's work-life a much less happy and fulfilling experience.

How a firm where harassment is common can educate its people to overcome this problem may be a difficult question. The first step might be the beginnings of a consensus among a section of the employees that something needs to be done to help the staff recognize the pain and damage caused by such practices, and to provide means of complaint and redress for those affected.

What might be done?
By employers
- What could you do:
  - about stereotypes?
  - about helping women to return to work?
  - about those with caring responsibilities (whether men or women)?

By local churches
- What could you do:
  - to support carers?
  - to overcome stereotypes?

By men
- What could you do:
  - to take a fair share of caring for the young and the old?
  - to overcome stereotypes in your own minds and in others' minds?

By women
- What could you do:
  - to further your own career?
  - to help other women to fulfilling work?
  - to share your caring responsibilities with others?

By Christians
- What can you do to discover God's will for you at work?

By all
- What could you do to discourage passive and active sexual harassment so far as it exists in your firm?

Prayer-notes

Experience How far is your workplace to some degree similar to many factories that a woman minister described: 'In many factories, men are patronizing to women; and I don't think they know they're doing it. It's the old traditional male superiority; and it's very difficult to get out of that. It took me a long time actually to stand up and be counted and say what I thought: that it was about seeing women not as stereotypes but as people'?

Pointers-to-depth Think of Jesus' meetings with men and women. How important was it to him to respond to people as the individuals they were?

Response How important is such a response to me?

'I don't think they know they're doing it.' Can you help people recognize the human reality in this matter?

Fifteen

Unemployed people

What is life like for an unemployed person?

'How nice not to work and to be paid for not doing so!' 'Most of them are unemployed because they're too idle to look for jobs!' 'A spell of unemployment doesn't normally do much harm.'

In fact these myths were exploded in 1982. A survey found that the strongest feelings of the great majority of the unemployed were, in order of strength, 'wondering whether they'll ever get a job, missing the company at work, getting very bored, feeling that any job is better than being out of work, and worrying about the effect it's having on other members of the family' (The Economist Intelligence Unit). The longer people are unemployed, the stronger those feelings get.

When a person loses a job, surveys have found, it is usually through bad luck. Two in three lose their job at a week's notice. 'Use your redundancy pay', a recent Prime Minister told them, 'and set up a business.' But in fact only one in ten get redundancy payments and few have savings to fall back on. Becoming unemployed means that income will normally be cut by at least a half.

Everyday experience for the unemployed is characterized by boredom. They find that their days and weeks no longer have a structure. Unless they have an engrossing hobby, they may have no productive activity. With regard to friends and neighbours, they see themselves as lacking status. Their social life is severely reduced through lack of money. Inside the family, tensions and arguments are common if the unemployment is long-term. It tends to lower the career aspirations of the unemployed person's children and lead them into occupations highly vulnerable to unemployment. Outside the family there is a narrowing circle of friends and decreasing contacts with them.

What are the prospects for an unemployed person? If the unemployment becomes long-term, employers will generally regard his or her job application with considerable wariness. If he or she does find a job, there is an even chance that it will be in a new line of work, where previous skills and experience will count for less. He or she will be liable to face a prospect of short-term jobs, at ever lower wages, interspersed by further periods of unemployment.

Who are unemployed people?

Two-thirds of unemployed people are under 35 with half their working life ahead of them. Only a minority are particularly handicapped within the labour market. So the unemployed are hardly distinguishable from other young people holding the lower-level jobs in our economy.

If someone becomes unemployed, that is not because he or she didn't bother to search for a job: 'All the attention and energies of the unemployed', a researcher found, 'were devoted to getting back into work', and fewer than 10 per cent turn down the chance of a job (W. Daniel). They are victims of circumstances in our society over which they have no control.

One of those circumstances is the loss of two million jobs in the UK manufacturing industry over the 1980s and the large rise of women seeking employment. Another is one of the worst education systems in Europe for fitting young people to the modern workplace. A third is our destructive class system which splits us into Us and Them, especially in the North, undermining the self-confidence and the trust of many in the workforce. A major consequence of that is that in whole areas young people are discouraged by their families and friends from further education and training, just when they are increasingly becoming the key to secure employment.

133

Unemployment mainly hits people who have low skills, and the average level of skills necessary for secure employment is steadily rising. The problem is becoming not unemployment but unemployability – except by those few companies that provide remedial education and training. So we cannot just wait for something to turn up. We must do something to bridge this gap.

Until we do that the number of long-term unemployed people is likely to remain at around 700,000, with perhaps half of that number out of work for more than three years.

What is being done?

The government funds an array of initiatives to try to tackle this problem and tries to adjust them in the light of experience. Some, like many Jobcentres, work well. Others could, with more local backing. But as things stand at present there are no signs that unemployment will diminish.

A hopeful sign you see in many localities is the growing tendency of companies to regard the development of their local community as something they need to get involved in for their long-term survival. Instead of just giving cash donations to worthy causes, they see the need to get involved in helping to tackle the problems we have been discussing. Most companies rate social responsibility as a very important motive (Ian Christie).

But how far do you find that your local employers try to avoid the common tendency of employers to screen out job applicants with an 'unemployment history'? In some areas we find this tendency being overcome through employers becoming involved in local schemes with the unemployed, an experience which has at least a chance of diminishing the stereotypes.

One of the most telling examples of what employers can do can be seen in a very deprived area of Glasgow where a firm connected with the Body Shop deliberately established itself in an area of high unemployment and, from the beginning, took job applicants as they came, without screening. This gesture to people who had lost hope generated great loyalty and commitment, with excellent results. But since that level of boldness is unlikely to become the norm, there will be a need for strategies like involving employers in overseeing Job Preparation courses.

When you look around in your area, you normally find that there are organizations and people there who want to get rid of this blight on the lives of so many people and who know that it is something we have to tackle together.

There are partnerships between local employers and other agencies for this purpose. There are also many local action groups who share the same goal. When you can put the churches together with all this, then you have a powerful mixture. This could lead to important local initiatives, perhaps something like the following:

1. The local authority not just reacting to closures but, with the co-operation of business, anticipating them and taking steps to mitigate their effects accordingly.
2. The local authority and/or firms considering promoting open-learning centres, which provide a better environment for gaining skills than courses for many of the people who need such help.
3. The provision of suitable counsellors – at present there are far too few of them.

What some local churches do

We have seen that for many long-term unemployed people, life without some job is a life without meaning. If we really believe that the life of a Christian consists in becoming involved, with Jesus, in God's compassionate, transforming love, we cannot 'pass by on the other side'. For that reason quite a number of local churches help tackle this human problem.

In some areas a church begins by taking careful soundings from the people professionally involved about where the employment gaps are in their area. 'If you decide to offer practical Christianity rather than theoretical Christianity, then you'll get a number of people on board who are interested', says the London Churches Employment Development Unit.

The church sets up a steering committee from these people. It invites on to the committee people who work professionally in the field and will know not just about the gaps but also about possibilities of follow-up.

Because of the great lack of jobs for people with low skills, the committee may set up a literacy or a basic office skills course, or it may seek to help other particularly disadvantaged groups like those with health problems or former prisoners.

The church will realize that it is important to get some local business people to join the committee, even though they will find it difficult to spare the time. Such people know what kinds of skills are needed and will make sure that the project is set up in such a way that it will deliver. Also, they may have a vested interest in funding some of the training.

It will probably be best to set up the project on a business-like financial basis. So the project will be costed out, on the basis of employing skilled and paid staff, and then necessary funds sought from various kinds of grants and donations. People will see it is being well run and will be more likely to help in different ways, including financially.

Michelle Rigby has had much experience of such projects and is enthusiastic: 'The whole church can be involved as the committee reports back and people can take an interest and rally round. It gives the church credibility in the area and a new identity.'

The results are likely to be even wider. The project will raise awareness and discussion of unemployment issues within the church, and this prompts more people to want to take action, either to help or to be helped.

As they begin to do so they will find that many projects already exist in the area which very few know about. They may be in skills training, or for helping people set up their own businesses, or pre-recruitment courses to increase people's self-confidence and job-readiness before interviews, for example. Or it may be the private initiatives of individuals. Many boroughs have home-tutoring schemes to help overcome illiteracy for those who cannot attend the set courses. Many home-tutors are in fact Christians who contact the local college and offer to help.

A huge and largely untapped source of Christian good-neighbourliness in this field lies in the small firms of the area. In the UK they have no co-ordination or voice. If every small firm in a locality just took on one of the disadvantaged categories, it would have an explosive effect.

What might be done?
By unemployed people
- You know that unemployment is a misfortune that can happen to any of us, but is experienced by most people

as deeply frustrating and painful. Can what we saw in
the first Part help you to get, nevertheless, something
positive out of your present situation: for yourself? for
others?

By all people

- Could you help to put the evil of unemployment more
  prominently on the national and local political agenda, so that
  politicians, business, the churches and others can collaborate
  to take steps to reduce it?
- Could you help some of the local unemployed people by
  getting involved in, or even helping to initiate, a local
  scheme?

By the local church

- Could your local church focus some of its energy on this
  matter? (Information about strategies that have worked for
  local churches is obtainable from either The London Churches
  Employment Development Unit, 45b Blythe Street, London
  E2 6LN (071–729 9990) or Linking-Up, 27 Blackfriars Road,
  Manchester M3 7AQ (061–832 5208).)

Prayer-notes

Experience Reflect on the feelings of unemployed people and
your response to them.

Pointers-to-depth Jesus unrolled the scroll and found the place
where it is written:

> The Spirit of the Lord is upon me,
> because he has chosen me to bring good news to the poor
> . . . to set free the oppressed
> and announce that the time has come
> when the Lord will save his people.
> (Luke 4:17–19)

The first contact of Christian love with social action is
. . . a 'simple uncomplicated compassion' which
spontaneously serves wherever it sees need. But if we see
a person in dire (misfortune), and we love that person,
there comes a time when that love must consider the
causes of the misery of the loved one – a time when love

not only binds the wounds but turns to stop the attack.
(Stephen Mott)

Response What could you do for unemployed people, either in spontaneous help or as part of a concerted effort to 'stop the attack' on millions of our compatriots?

Sixteen

Ethnic discrimination

When we face a complex human problem we need time to cope with it. We have to get through not only to the facts but also to the emotions of those deeply involved, including our own. Then we have to try to see them in perspective before we decide what to do.

In the matter of ethnic discrimination, it is only relatively recently that most of us began to try to confront the problem. In the 1980s, a survey found that there was a 'dramatic increase in public awareness of race issues' and a recognition that black people suffer from 'acute disadvantages'. So far very little has been done to reduce those disadvantages. How can we find our way to harnessing our new awareness?

Before trying to see what we could do, particularly in our local situations, we may like to recall what those 'acute disadvantages' consist of.

What is the problem?

In a survey of young unemployed people in Britain, we read that 'young Asian men and young Afro-Caribbean women had among the highest qualification levels, and the lowest chances of getting jobs' (Michael White and Susan McRae). We know that the same problem exists in most other countries.

Consider those of us who are members of ethnic communities. It is not easy for us to avoid feelings of resentment. Already we have the insecurity that comes from not being fully 'owned' by our own country. And those higher qualifications don't come easily – especially since some teachers tend to allocate us to the less motivated sets and classes.

Although most people in this country are not happy with this injustice, desire for justice has so far brought little change. The unemployment rate for black people is nearly twice that of white people. Even black graduates are disadvantaged in obtaining jobs and in getting training and promotion. It seems to make no difference that it has been shown that once they are established they do at least as well as white graduates.

It is encouraging that the main cause of this discrimination is something that could be changed: employers' preconceived image of black people's unsuitableness. They have a picture of a white person, who would do the job in the way that they themselves would. They find it difficult to take on board the possibility that someone from a different culture might do it, perhaps differently, but at least as well.

It is also encouraging to know that some firms are helping their managers to tackle this difficulty. It is heartening to see, in many countries and in Britain, major organizations like British Rail encouraging their managers to analyse their own race conditioning. National institutions like London Underground, Rover, Ford, and even the police in some areas, are also helping to create a wave. But that wave, alas, is as yet so small. How small? *The Equal Opportunities Review* said that in 1989 TSB Bank was 'among the few companies which are actively taking steps to recruit ethnic minorities'.

Being prime victims of unemployment is the worst disadvantage of ethnic minorities. It can make them feel that they are rejected for unfair reasons and more cut off from the mainstream. It can breed in their children a feeling of hopelessness and resentment.

Need this be?

When white people open their minds and hearts to that experience of the ethnic communities, few want that kind of life for anyone. What helps many tolerate it is that this kind of life is discreetly hidden from them by city architects. Except for those of us who live or work there, few people visit inner cities or deprived housing estates.

Over the next ten years, what do we want to happen?

What many white people have tended to do, normally without thinking about it, is to keep these communities at arm's length. Sometimes that takes the form of implicitly assuming that it is up to others to change their life-style if they want equal opportunities. This can come over to the ethnic communities, especially their younger members, as 'Forget your communities and the inherited memories that are your life blood. Forget your feelings of belonging and your sense of meaning. If you want to be treated as citizens of this country, you will have to be like us.'

There is another way in which, again usually not deliberately, ethnic communities can feel that they are being kept at arm's length. There the message they pick up is: 'You can have your assemblies in our schools. You can even study your own religion there and dress as you want. We'll even try to diminish the discrimination against you. Go ahead. Do your own thing. But don't bother us.'

It is easy to understand the effect of these implicit messages, however unintentional, on, say, an Asian or Afro-Caribbean boy or girl. Inevitably they will feel that the general attitude is one of suspicion or distaste of their ways of feeling and living.

If this impasse continues, it is not difficult to predict the consequences. It will heighten the feelings of insecurity and of being marginalized, especially in children and young adults. It will throttle the vitality and the regenerative power of those communities. And, among white people, it will provide inadequate incentive to overcome discrimination. We can imagine the situation if we leave things as they are.

Few of us need books to tell us that there is an alternative. In our local shops and restaurants, in holiday travel, sport and music, we have enjoyed kinds of vitality and customs different from our own. We may have felt enriched by the experience.

So, could we overcome negative messages – however undeliberate – between white and black and show pride and delight even in our differences? Of course that isn't easy when the issue is living together in spite of differences. But the decisive factor is how strong is our motivation to try to overcome the difficulties. That will depend on our vision of our country for the next decade or two.

Could our country learn to take pride and joy in a greater variety of cultures? Could we move away from the stereotype of a uniform culture so as to give affirmation and welcome to different cultures?

That would allow us all to develop richly, joyfully and with confidence, and with a feeling of being a valued part of the society in which we live.

The deepest problem that still faces us may be that, on the whole, people are most at ease with other people like themselves. It is with regard to this last problem that our Christian faith can offer special help. In our first chapter we recalled that Christianity, when it is true to itself, sees itself as serving the one human story. The most moving indication of that is what St Paul lets us see about the experiences of becoming a Christian in the churches he founded. It was of the overcoming of all the deepest aspects of human divisiveness. For those clothed with the life of Christ, 'there is neither Jew nor Greek, slave nor free, male nor female' (Galatians 3:28). Baptism was a commitment to, and a promise of, humanity's dream and destiny of eventual reunification.

We do need and enjoy our own families, our groups and communities: we need that look *inwards*. But, for our human life to come to fullness, we also need the look *outwards*. We need to open ourselves to the variety and the ultimate unity of our human story. How much in modern history shows us that that is not easy, but no less necessary!

Our Christianity should also remind us that this story is about humanity, not a theory. What this story consists of is our responding to this hugely varied body of human beings, who are *all* by nature loving and lovable. The only ultimately serious choice that confronts any of us is the one between saying, with our lives, 'yes' or 'no' to the men and women around us as our faith helps us to see them. All depends on our 'letting love make you serve one another'. 'If you sow in the field of the Spirit, you will gather the harvest of eternal life' (Galatians 5:13; 6:8).

Keeping people at arm's length is the antithesis of love. Welcoming their lovableness joyfully is what our faith and our humanity urge on us.

What is being done?

At a discussion dinner of directors of major companies four years ago, few were satisfied with their achievements in recruiting black people. What, then, are the obstacles? And what is being done to overcome them?

The most obvious obstacle lies in the method of recruitment. 'Employers seemed interested during interviews', said a black 17-year-old, 'and they were certainly not hostile. But they always went for the white applicants' (*Financial Times* article).

The reason for this is not usually *deliberate* racism. The interviewer has probably had no help even to recognize his or her instinctive discrimination, and most companies have no idea that their recruitment from the ethnic communities is so small.

Experience has shown that these problems can be successfully overcome by using several measures. A firm could begin by checking its own proportion of such recruitment against the proportion of black people in the locality or nationally. In the light of that it can set itself long-term targets. It will obviously need to train its recruiters in avoiding discrimination. Then it may consider how it treats applicants from the ethnic communities. They may lack self-confidence, and all candidates could probably benefit from a less complex application form.

A further step is to establish a good relationship with the local schools and community centres – Rover has again pointed the way by encouraging its black trainees to give talks to prospective applicants in both those settings. It will also be necessary to deal with the fact that 42 per cent of job vacancies are filled by informal methods, so that many vacancies never get known to the ethnic communities. Any firm can find ways of reducing that obstacle if it wishes.

The best context in which a firm can take such steps is a general equal opportunity programme which it has led the work force to be happy with. One advantage would be that that should encourage trade union support. The question is whether more than a small minority of firms will take such steps. 'In the private sector', researchers wrote, 'we were told repeatedly by informants that a business reason is required for all decisions, and that a simple argument about justice has little effect' (Colin Brown and Jean Lawton). There *are* business reasons that can often be pointed to, like fears of recruitment shortages and fears of a poor image with the ethnic community in a firm's area.

Through a mixture of law, promotion and persuasion that motivation must be broadened. The churches and their members could greatly assist that.

What might be done?
By all of us

- Whether you are white or from an ethnic community, could you take steps to get to know better the people and values of some different communities?
- Could you encourage such initiatives also in your local schools?
- Could you look at the unemployment situation of the ethnic minorities in your area and the local firms' policies for recruiting from them?
- Could you look at the local situation with regard to harassment?
- Since we know that the best way of getting to know people is to share some activity with them, could you share in one with members of an ethnic community?

By employers and senior management

- Could you monitor the proportion of black people you employ against local or national levels?
- Could you negotiate and then institute an equal opportunity policy in your firm?
- Could you revise your recruitment methods accordingly?
- Could you help to make the local ethnic communities feel welcome and a valued part of local life?

By local churches

- Could you ensure that members of ethnic minorities feel welcome and valued, not just in the church buildings, but also in the church's life and decision-making processes?
- Could you look carefully at the manner of worship and ask whether it is truly inclusive and valuing of everybody?
- Could you consider providing, perhaps with others, facilities like English language training for Asian workers, if there is a need for some such facilities in your area?

Books etc. referred to

John Adair, 'Take Me to Your Leader', *Director* (November 1988).

John Baker, 'A Summary and Synthesis' in G. Limouris (ed.), *Church, Kingdom, World* (World Council of Churches, 1986); quoted in David Bosch, below.

Warren Bennis, *The Unconscious Conspiracy* (American Management Association, 1976).

David Bosch, *Transforming Mission* (Orbis Books, 1991).

Breadline Britain 1990s: The Findings of the Television Series (Domino Films/LWT, 1991).

Colin Brown and Jean Lawton, *Training for Equality* (Policy Studies Institute, 1991).

Peter Carnley, *The Structure of Resurrection Belief* (OUP, 1987).

Ian Christie *et al.*, *Profitable Partnerships* (Policy Studies Institute, 1991).

Gillian Dalley (ed.), *Disability and Social Policy* (Policy Studies Institute, 1991).

W. Daniel, *The Unemployed Flow* (Policy Studies Institute, 1991).

Max De Pree, *Leadership Is an Art* (Doubleday, 1989).

The Economist Intelligence Unit, *Coping with Unemployment: The Effects on the Unemployed Themselves* (Economist Intelligence Unit, 1982).

Frank Glendenning (ed.), *Care in the Community* (London, 1982).

J. C. Hoekendijk, *The Church Inside Out* (SCM Press, 1967).

John Paul II, Encyclical *Redemptoris Missio* on the Church's missionary mandate (1991).

Peter Laslett, *A Fresh Map of Life* (Weidenfeld & Nicolson, 1989).

Richard McBrien, quoted in Edward J. Dunn, *Missionary Theology* (University of America Press, 1980).

Stephen Mott, *Biblical Ethics and Social Change* (OUP, 1982).

Stephen Pilling, *Rehabilitation and Community Care* (Routledge, 1991).

Karl Rahner, *Theological Investigations* 6 (Darton, Longman & Todd, 1969).

Michael White, *Against Unemployment* (Policy Studies Institute, 1991).

Michael White and Susan McRae, *Young Adults and Long-Term Unemployment* (Policy Studies Institute, 1989).

Faith in the World

Edmund Flood, with others, is publishing for piloting early in 1993 a parish programme, *Faith in Life*, that aims to stimulate people's awareness of their calling in daily life – at work, at home and leisure, as volunteers and as members of the community – and to see this as the field in which they are doing God's work as lay apostles.

This year-long process enables individuals, groups and parishes to reflect on the way the good news interacts with the whole of their lives. It is an ecumenical whole-parish process which helps people to reflect on what they may do and so encourages a closer relationship between life, faith, the Christian community and the world beyond the church doors.

It aims to assist local churches

- to identify their mission in their own local context in relation to the life and work of their local community especially the social, economic and cultural dimensions;
- to enable their members (and others) to identify their own vocation and mission in all dimensions of daily life and activity especially in the activity which they mainly do whether paid work or some other kind of work;
- by ecumenical formation based on small groups and following the pastoral cycle method;

- by liturgical celebration, events and activities to raise the awareness of the whole parish community;
- through practical activities, projects and strategies;
- through development of relationships/alliances with other local churches, community groups, agencies and employers.

Dioceses, parishes and organizations would commit themselves to a year-long process in three parts:

Preparation (Easter to autumn)
First Session (six weeks between autumn and Christmas)
Second Session (six weeks between Christmas and Easter)

It is expected that participation will result in action of some kind, whether individual or corporate, or in a new attitude to action which is already taking place.

For further information:
All Church Series
Ealing Abbey
London W5 2DY